How To Make Books With Children

Joy Evans & Jo Ellen Moore

Table of Contents

HOW TO MAKE BOOKS WITH CHILDREN

One of the greatest motivational techniques for encouraging students at any grade level to write is to provide many opportunities for sharing their stories with others. In this resource book we provide directions, patterns, forms and writing ideas to create dozens of different books — enough to fill a class library with books written and illustrated by your own students.

How to Make Books With Children helps with:

1. Motivation
   Create a feeling of excitement and satisfaction about writing and sharing stories. You will find your students re-reading their own stories over and over again, as well as those of their classmates.

2. Creative Expression
   Develop skills in writing stories, descriptive paragraphs, poetry, and special themes such as alphabet books and riddle books.

3. Practicing Skills
   What better way is there to practice writing skills than by the experience of frequently writing one's own stories? The knowledge that their work will be read by others encourages children to use complete sentences, interesting words, correct punctuation and spelling, and to stick to the main idea.

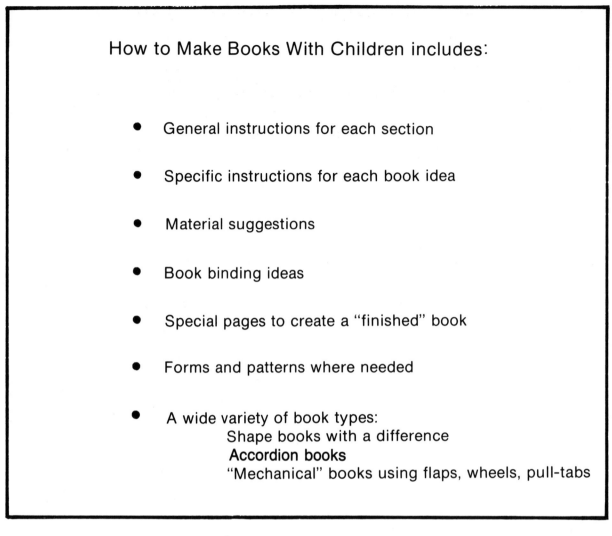

How to Make Books With Children includes:

- General instructions for each section

- Specific instructions for each book idea

- Material suggestions

- Book binding ideas

- Special pages to create a "finished" book

- Forms and patterns where needed

- A wide variety of book types:
  Shape books with a difference
  Accordion books
  "Mechanical" books using flaps, wheels, pull-tabs

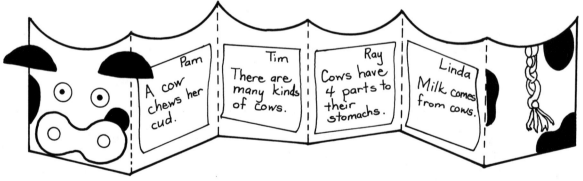

Now that you've created these wonderful books, why not let others have a chance to see them? Of course you want to put them in your class library, but why not ask for a space in the school library, so that other classes might have a chance to read them? Invite parents to a "book show." They will be as delighted as your new authors.

The suggestions we provide are just a beginning. Let your imagination and those of your students soar. You will be surprised and delighted at what you all can create.

NOTE: If you feel the need for more specific steps in the writing stage of creating books, see *Creative Writing Ideas* published by EVAN-MOOR in 1984.

PUTTING A BOOK TOGETHER

front
cover

title
page

dedication
page

story

about
the
author

back
cover

Attach Story Pages

- Pages may simply be stapled together before being put into a cover.

- Pages may be glued to a backing of construction paper, then stapled together and covered.

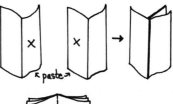

- Pages may be folded in half, then glued back-to-back. This is necessary for book forms such as pop-up pages.

- Pages may be folded and then stitched down the center. Stitching may be done on a machine or by hand with darning needles.

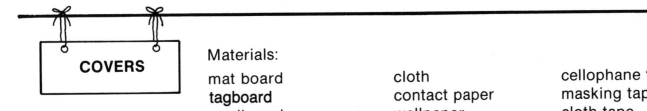

COVERS

Materials:

mat board	cloth	cellophane tape
tagboard	contact paper	masking tape
cardboard	wallpaper	cloth tape
construction paper	wrapping paper	duct tape

If you create a class book, select one student to illustrate the cover before attaching it to the book.

Always cut cover pieces larger than the writing paper. ¼ to ½ inch is usually enough.

Don't forget to include a title page, etc. for "special books."

Quick and Easy These covers require little time to create.

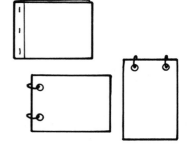

1. Staple cover to stories. Cover the staples with a strip of tape.

2. Punch holes through the cover and stories. Put together with metal rings.

Or tie with shoe laces, yarn, or string.

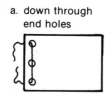
a. down through end holes

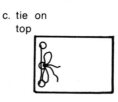
b. up through middle hole

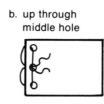
c. tie on top

Hinged Covers

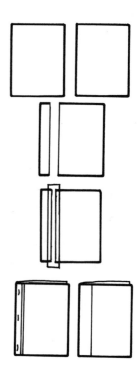

Cut two pieces of tagboard, cardboard, etc. slightly larger than the story pages.

Cut ½ inch strip from the left hand side of the front cover.

Tape the strips together on the inside. Leave an ⅛" space open between the two strips.

Staple cover and story pages together. Cover the front hinge and the front and back staples with a 1 1/2 inch piece of cloth/book tape.

Folded Tag Cover (for pages glued back to back)

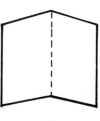

Cut colored tag slightly larger than the story pages. Score the center and fold. Rub firmly.

Paste the story pages back to back. (See page 3 for directions.) Add an empty page to the front and back of your story to serve as end pages. Paste the end pages to the cover.

This cover can only be used for books containing no more than 6-10 pages. Any more are difficult to handle.

4

Cloth Cover

Cut two pieces of cardboard slightly larger than the story pages.

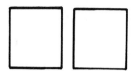

Place the cardboard on a piece of cloth about 1-1½ inches larger than the cover. Leave a small space in between the cover pieces.

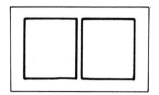

Miter the corners of the fabric.

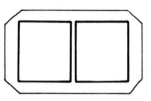

Place diluted white glue on the cloth and fold over the cover.

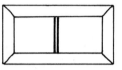

Story pages should be cut almost the length of the cover. Stitch 4-6 pages together down the center with a darning needle and thread or a sewing machine.

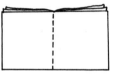

Leave the first and last pages empty to serve as end papers. Write and illustrate the story. Paste the end papers to the cover to complete the book.

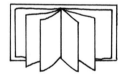

SPECIAL PAGES

These pages can be done as guided writing activities with your class using the same paper as the story is written on or by using the forms on pages 6-7.

- **Title page** — include the title, author, illustrator, room number, and school.

  - Dedication page—dedicate your story to someone special to you or someone who has helped you in some way.

    - About the Author—describe yourself. Tell about your likes and dislikes. You may want to tell why you chose the subject of your story.

Sample Title Page

_____

Title

_____

Author

_____

Illustrator

_____

Publisher

_____

Date

I dedicate this book to

About the Author

picture

SHAPE BOOKS

Shape books are not just for primary children. We have included some interesting variations to make them motivating for older students also.

- "Regular" where the front and back covers are the same.

 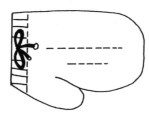

- "Add an element" such as legs, tails, or zippers!

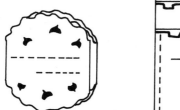  

- "Three part fold-outs" of houses, caves, cookies!

 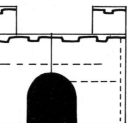

All are quickly prepared following simple formats. They can be used for group books where writing is a phrase, sentence, or short story or for longer stories written by individuals. Size of the shape cover can be varied to fit the type of writing paper you prefer to use.

Each book idea provides specific directions for creating the cover and several writing suggestions for that cover.

Read all directions before you begin. In the primary grades, the teacher will need to prepare the covers and cut the paper to shape. Older students can create their own covers using a template and following the direction sheet.

Draw the basic shape on construction paper or on tag for your cover and on writing paper of your choice for the writing activity.

cover

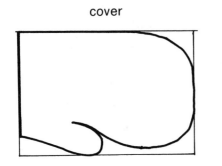

trace on 2 sheets of tag or construction paper for front and back covers

writing paper

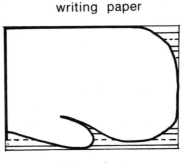

trace and cut out as many sheets as are needed by your class

put pages together

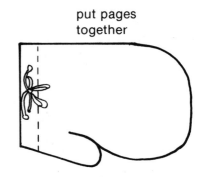

staple pages or use a hole punch, then tie together

You may wish to select a child to decorate the cover if it is to be a group book. Also, laminated covers last longer for books that will be used often.

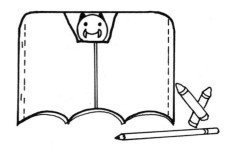

Three part fold-out books will need paper cut to fit the center section.

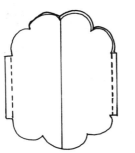

Several writing papers can be stapled in place for longer stories.

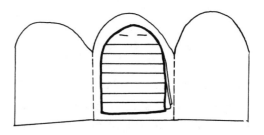

The Mitten Book

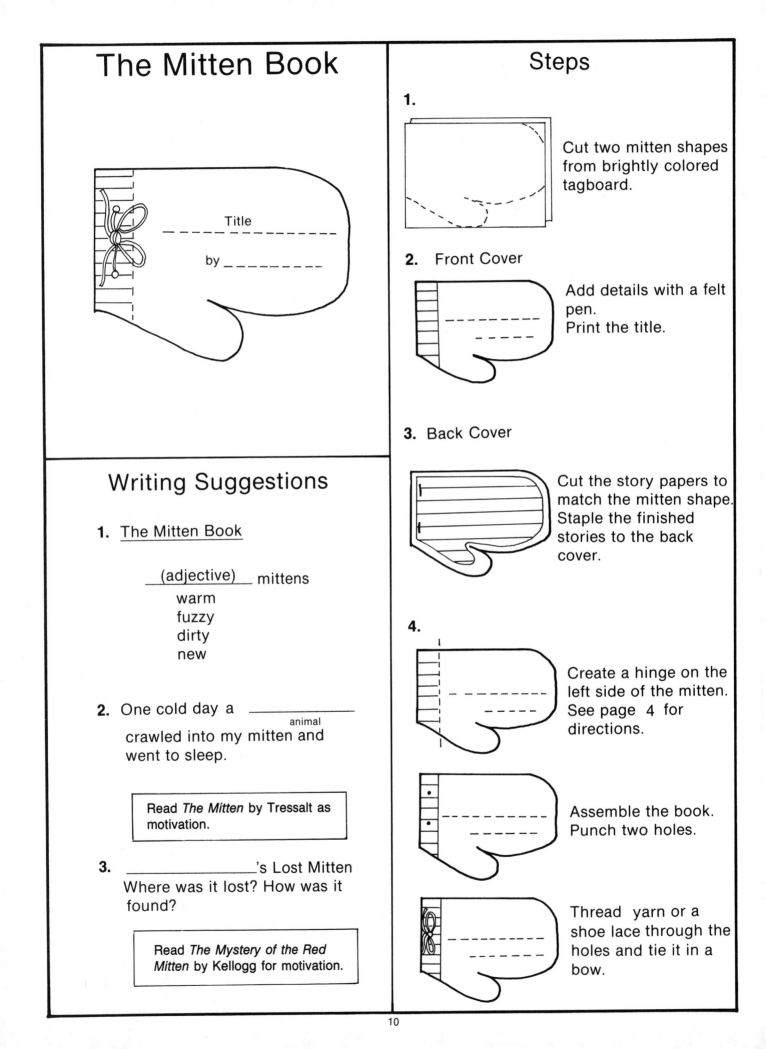

Title
- - - - - - - - - - -

by - - - - - - - - -

Steps

1. Cut two mitten shapes from brightly colored tagboard.

2. Front Cover

Add details with a felt pen.
Print the title.

3. Back Cover

Cut the story papers to match the mitten shape. Staple the finished stories to the back cover.

4. Create a hinge on the left side of the mitten. See page 4 for directions.

Assemble the book. Punch two holes.

Thread yarn or a shoe lace through the holes and tie it in a bow.

Writing Suggestions

1. The Mitten Book

___(adjective)___ mittens
warm
fuzzy
dirty
new

2. One cold day a _____
                        animal
crawled into my mitten and went to sleep.

> Read *The Mitten* by Tressalt as motivation.

3. _____'s Lost Mitten
Where was it lost? How was it found?

> Read *The Mystery of the Red Mitten* by Kellogg for motivation.

A Zipper Book

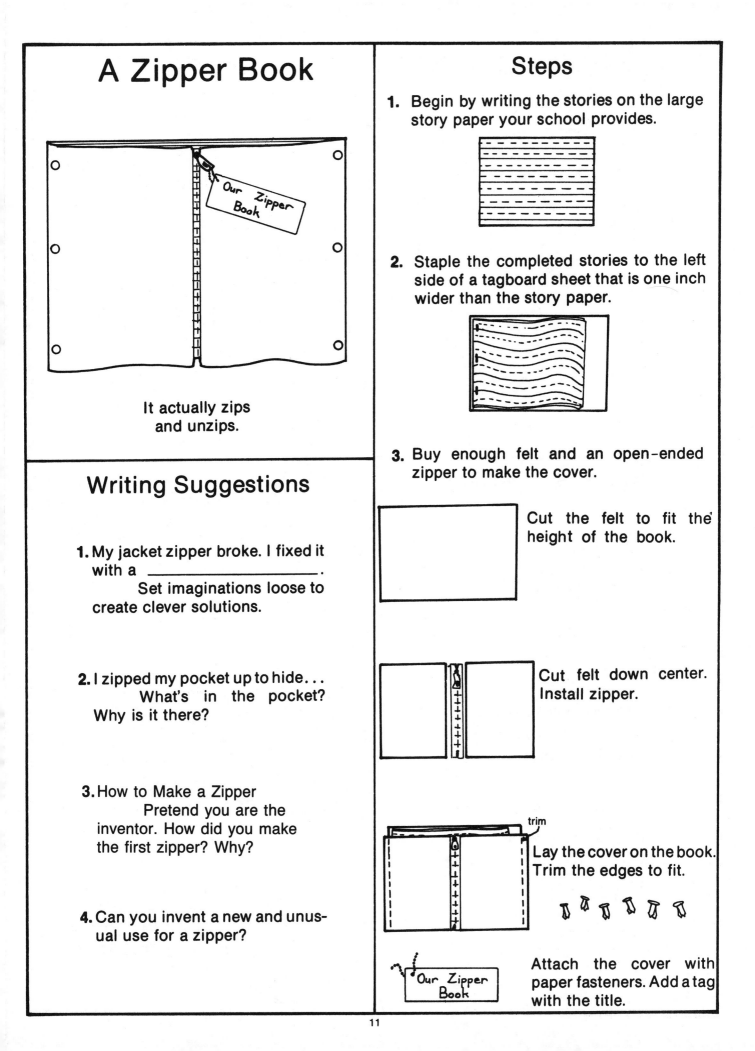

It actually zips
and unzips.

Writing Suggestions

1. My jacket zipper broke. I fixed it with a _____.
   Set imaginations loose to create clever solutions.

2. I zipped my pocket up to hide...
   What's in the pocket? Why is it there?

3. How to Make a Zipper
   Pretend you are the inventor. How did you make the first zipper? Why?

4. Can you invent a new and unusual use for a zipper?

Steps

1. Begin by writing the stories on the large story paper your school provides.

2. Staple the completed stories to the left side of a tagboard sheet that is one inch wider than the story paper.

3. Buy enough felt and an open-ended zipper to make the cover.

Cut the felt to fit the height of the book.

Cut felt down center. Install zipper.

Lay the cover on the book. Trim the edges to fit.

Attach the cover with paper fasteners. Add a tag with the title.

Phases of the Moon

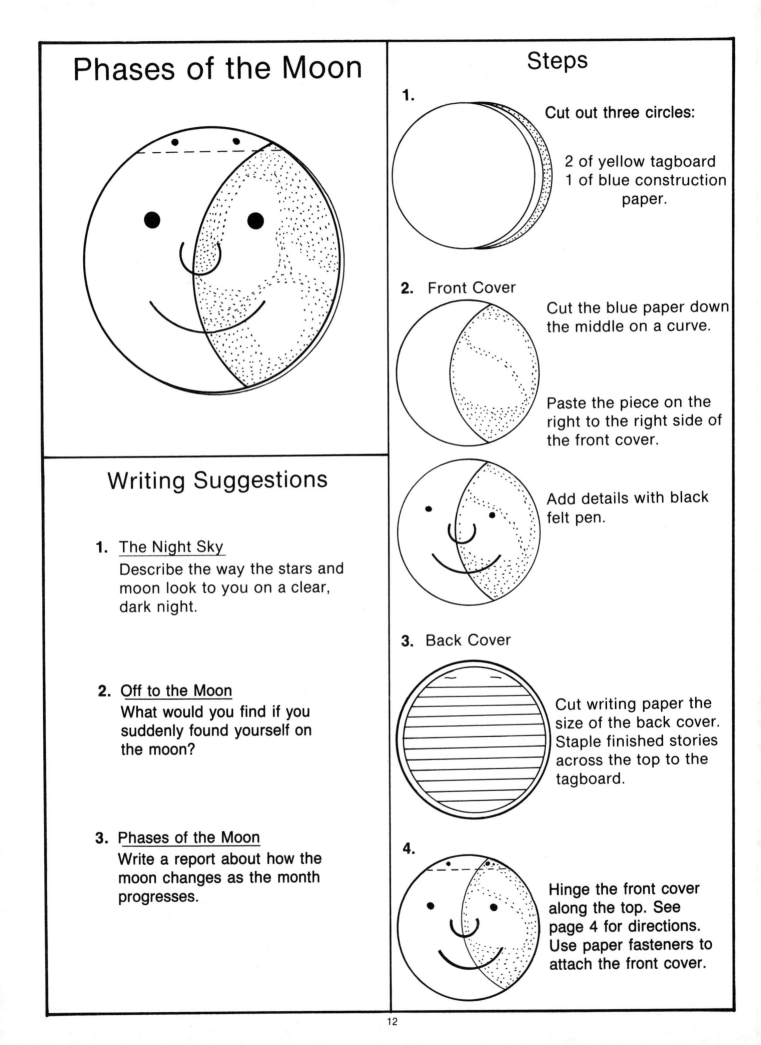

Steps

1. Cut out three circles:

2 of yellow tagboard
1 of blue construction
paper.

2. Front Cover

Cut the blue paper down
the middle on a curve.

Paste the piece on the
right to the right side of
the front cover.

Add details with black
felt pen.

3. Back Cover

Cut writing paper the
size of the back cover.
Staple finished stories
across the top to the
tagboard.

4.

Hinge the front cover
along the top. See
page 4 for directions.
Use paper fasteners to
attach the front cover.

Writing Suggestions

1. <u>The Night Sky</u>
Describe the way the stars and
moon look to you on a clear,
dark night.

2. <u>Off to the Moon</u>
What would you find if you
suddenly found yourself on
the moon?

3. <u>Phases of the Moon</u>
Write a report about how the
moon changes as the month
progresses.

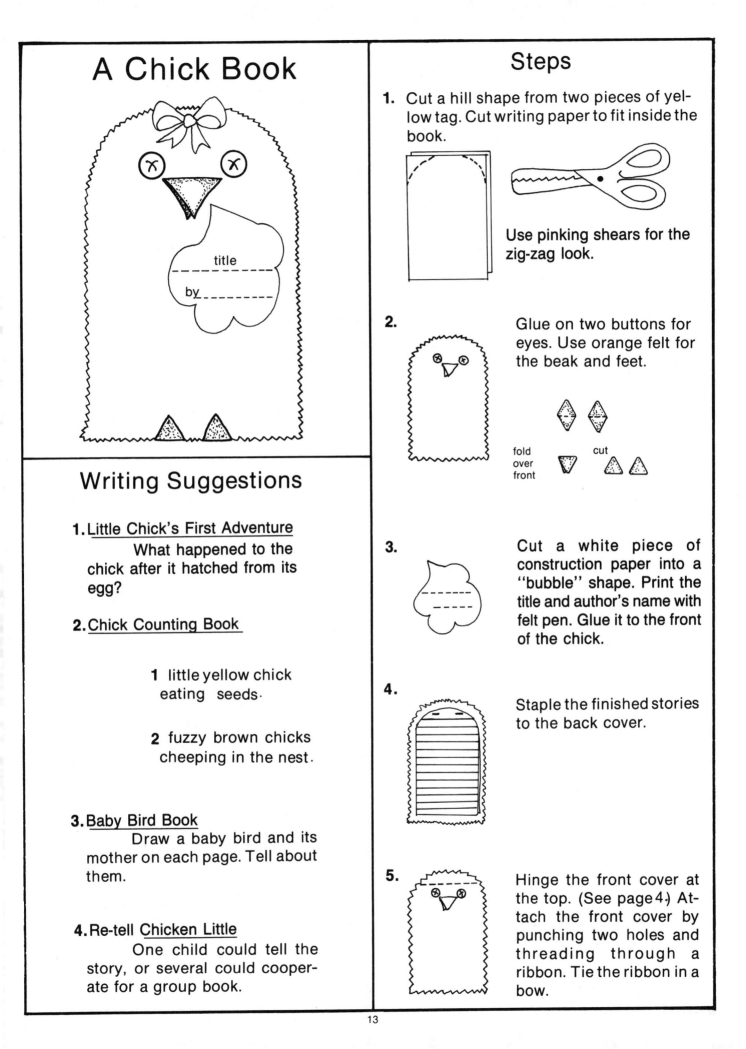

A Chick Book

title
by

Writing Suggestions

1. Little Chick's First Adventure
What happened to the chick after it hatched from its egg?

2. Chick Counting Book

1 little yellow chick eating seeds.

2 fuzzy brown chicks cheeping in the nest.

3. Baby Bird Book
Draw a baby bird and its mother on each page. Tell about them.

4. Re-tell Chicken Little
One child could tell the story, or several could cooperate for a group book.

Steps

1. Cut a hill shape from two pieces of yellow tag. Cut writing paper to fit inside the book.

Use pinking shears for the zig-zag look.

2. Glue on two buttons for eyes. Use orange felt for the beak and feet.

fold over front   cut

3. Cut a white piece of construction paper into a "bubble" shape. Print the title and author's name with felt pen. Glue it to the front of the chick.

4. Staple the finished stories to the back cover.

5. Hinge the front cover at the top. (See page 4.) Attach the front cover by punching two holes and threading through a ribbon. Tie the ribbon in a bow.

A Fish Book

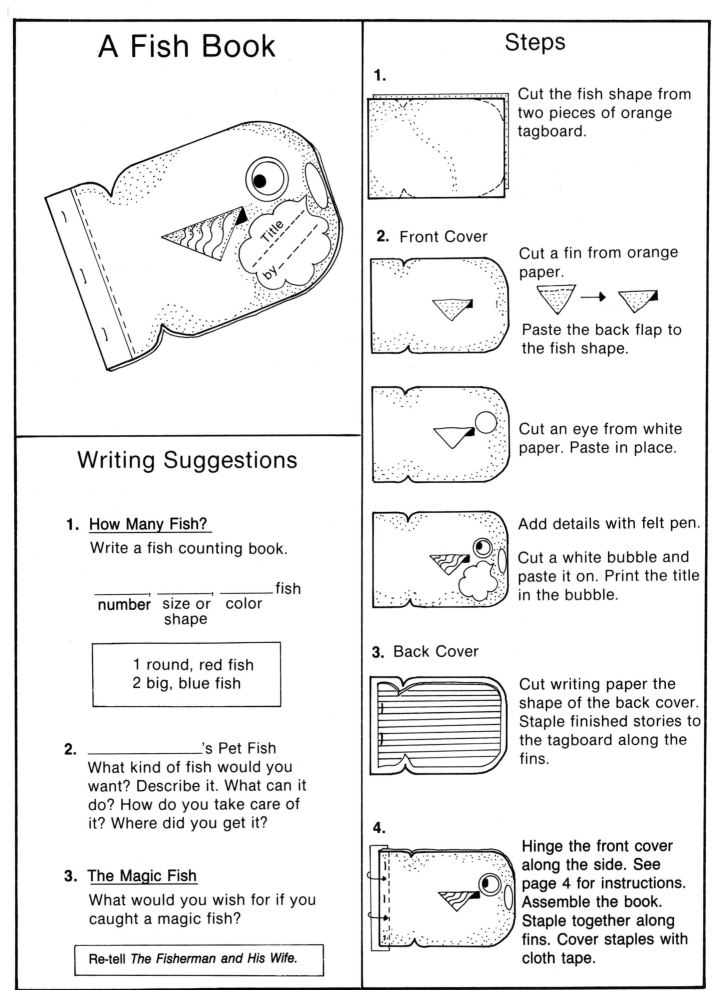

Writing Suggestions

1. <u>How Many Fish?</u>

Write a fish counting book.

———— , ———— , ————fish
number   size or   color
          shape

| 1 round, red fish |
| 2 big, blue fish |

2. _____'s Pet Fish
What kind of fish would you want? Describe it. What can it do? How do you take care of it? Where did you get it?

3. <u>The Magic Fish</u>

What would you wish for if you caught a magic fish?

Re-tell *The Fisherman and His Wife.*

Steps

1.

Cut the fish shape from two pieces of orange tagboard.

2. Front Cover

Cut a fin from orange paper.

Paste the back flap to the fish shape.

Cut an eye from white paper. Paste in place.

Add details with felt pen.

Cut a white bubble and paste it on. Print the title in the bubble.

3. Back Cover

Cut writing paper the shape of the back cover. Staple finished stories to the tagboard along the fins.

4.

Hinge the front cover along the side. See page 4 for instructions. Assemble the book. Staple together along fins. Cover staples with cloth tape.

The Bus Book

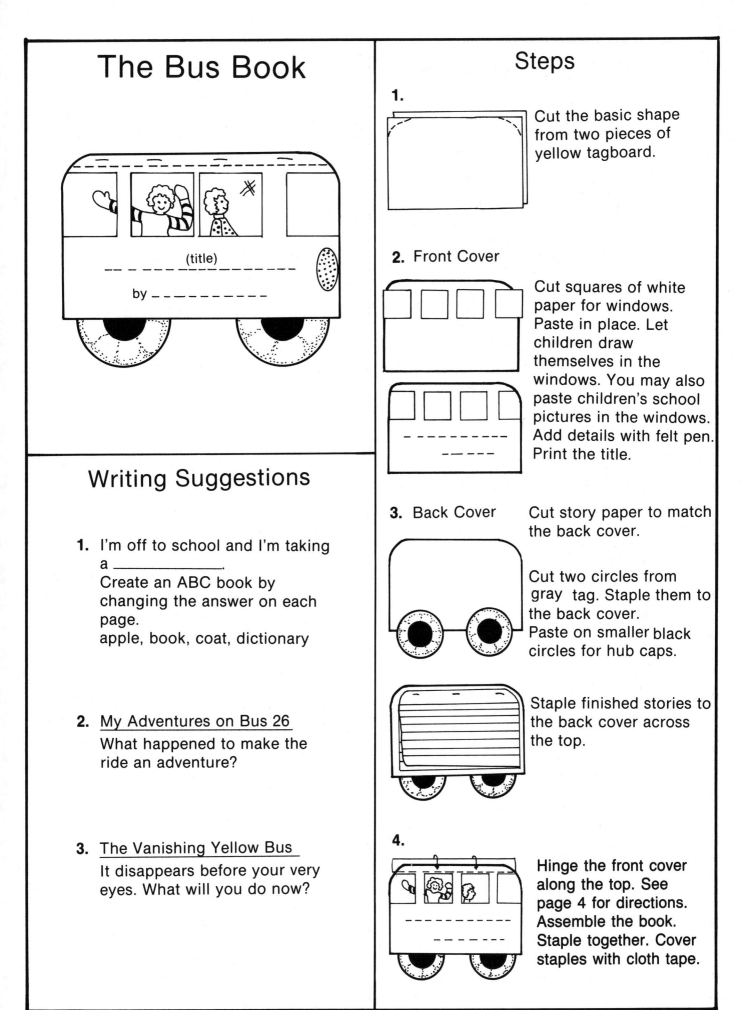

---- (title) ----
----
by -----------

Writing Suggestions

1. I'm off to school and I'm taking
a _____.
Create an ABC book by
changing the answer on each
page.
apple, book, coat, dictionary

2. <u>My Adventures on Bus 26</u>
What happened to make the
ride an adventure?

3. <u>The Vanishing Yellow Bus</u>
It disappears before your very
eyes. What will you do now?

Steps

1.
Cut the basic shape
from two pieces of
yellow tagboard.

2. Front Cover

Cut squares of white
paper for windows.
Paste in place. Let
children draw
themselves in the
windows. You may also
paste children's school
pictures in the windows.
Add details with felt pen.
Print the title.

3. Back Cover

Cut story paper to match
the back cover.

Cut two circles from
gray tag. Staple them to
the back cover.
Paste on smaller black
circles for hub caps.

Staple finished stories to
the back cover across
the top.

4.

Hinge the front cover
along the top. See
page 4 for directions.
Assemble the book.
Staple together. Cover
staples with cloth tape.

A Robot Book

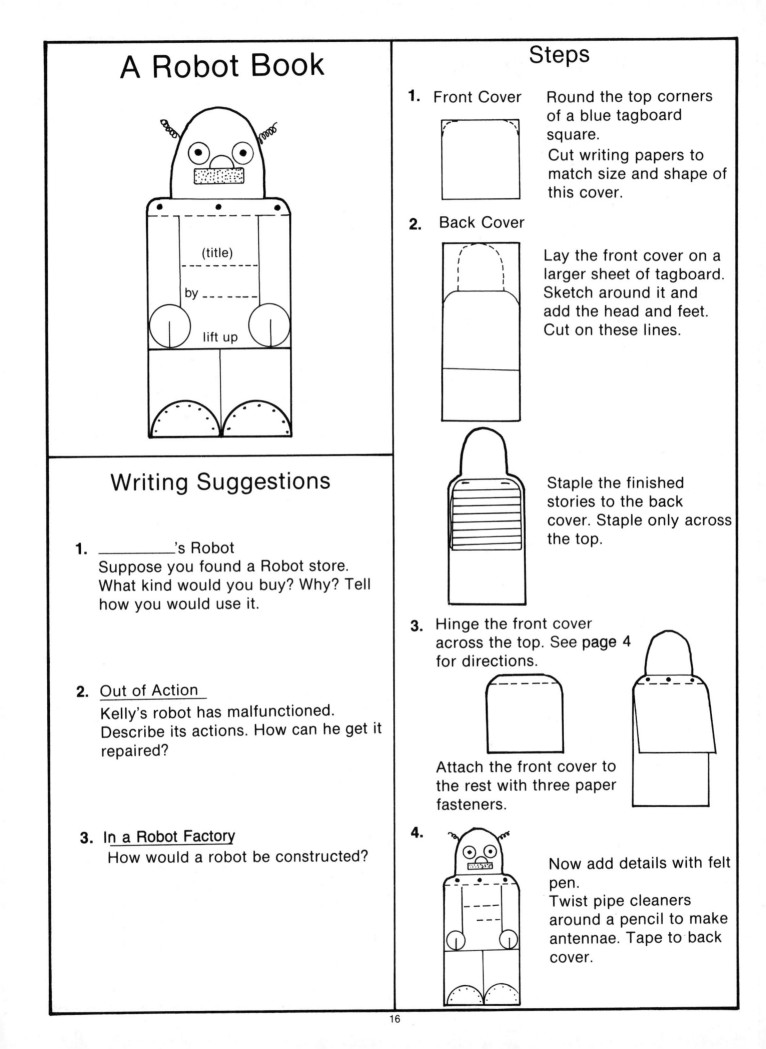

(title)

by _ _ _ _ _

lift up

Writing Suggestions

1. _____'s Robot
   Suppose you found a Robot store. What kind would you buy? Why? Tell how you would use it.

2. Out of Action
   Kelly's robot has malfunctioned. Describe its actions. How can he get it repaired?

3. In a Robot Factory
   How would a robot be constructed?

Steps

1. Front Cover — Round the top corners of a blue tagboard square.
   Cut writing papers to match size and shape of this cover.

2. Back Cover

   Lay the front cover on a larger sheet of tagboard. Sketch around it and add the head and feet. Cut on these lines.

   Staple the finished stories to the back cover. Staple only across the top.

3. Hinge the front cover across the top. See **page 4** for directions.

   Attach the front cover to the rest with three paper fasteners.

4. Now add details with felt pen.
   Twist pipe cleaners around a pencil to make antennae. Tape to back cover.

A Bunny Book

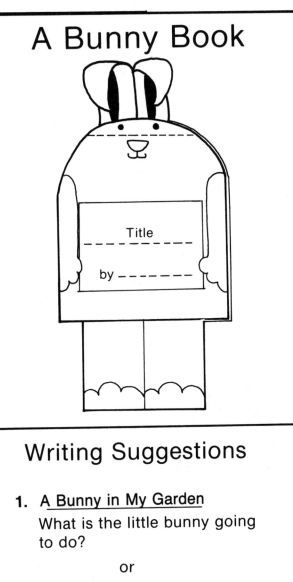

Title

by _ _ _ _ _

Writing Suggestions

1. <u>A Bunny in My Garden</u>
What is the little bunny going to do?

or

Re-tell *Peter Rabbit* in your own words.

2. <u>The Tricky Hare</u>
He is after the seeds for giant carrots. Will he be able to get them? Will he be caught first?

3. <u>Adventures of a Cottontail</u>
What happens when a rabbit goes out into the world for the first time?

Steps

1. Front Cover

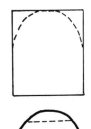

Round the corners of a white tagboard rectangle.

Glue on a piece of pink paper.

2. Back Cover

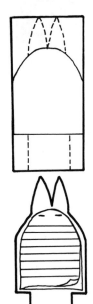

Lay the front cover on a larger sheet of tagboard. Sketch around it and add the ears and feet. Cut on these lines.

Cut writing papers to match the size and shape of the front cover.

Staple the finished stories to the back cover. Staple only across the top.

3.

Hinge the front cover across the top. See page 4 for directions.
Attach the front cover to the rest with two paper fasteners. These are also the Bunny's eyes.

4.

Add details with felt pens: fuzzy feet, pink ears, arms, pink nose. Curl the ears forward. Print the title.

The Owl Book

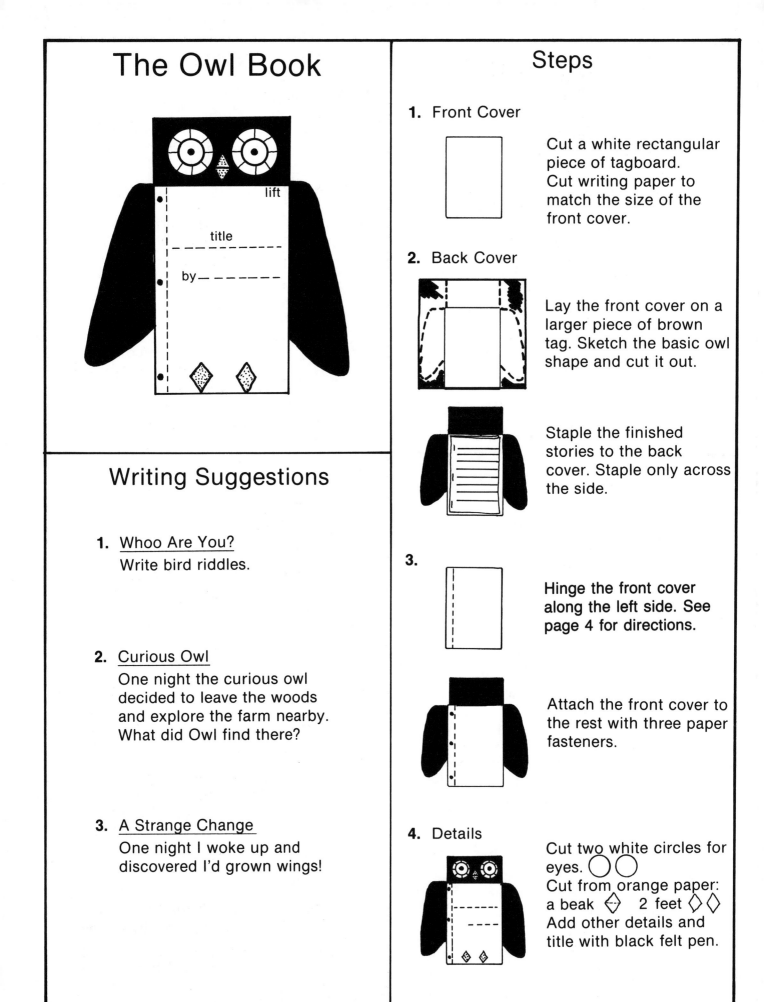

lift

title

by

Writing Suggestions

1. <u>Whoo Are You?</u>
Write bird riddles.

2. <u>Curious Owl</u>
One night the curious owl decided to leave the woods and explore the farm nearby. What did Owl find there?

3. <u>A Strange Change</u>
One night I woke up and discovered I'd grown wings!

Steps

1. Front Cover

Cut a white rectangular piece of tagboard. Cut writing paper to match the size of the front cover.

2. Back Cover

Lay the front cover on a larger piece of brown tag. Sketch the basic owl shape and cut it out.

Staple the finished stories to the back cover. Staple only across the side.

3.

Hinge the front cover along the left side. See page 4 for directions.

Attach the front cover to the rest with three paper fasteners.

4. Details

Cut two white circles for eyes.
Cut from orange paper: a beak 2 feet
Add other details and title with black felt pen.

18

A Frog Book

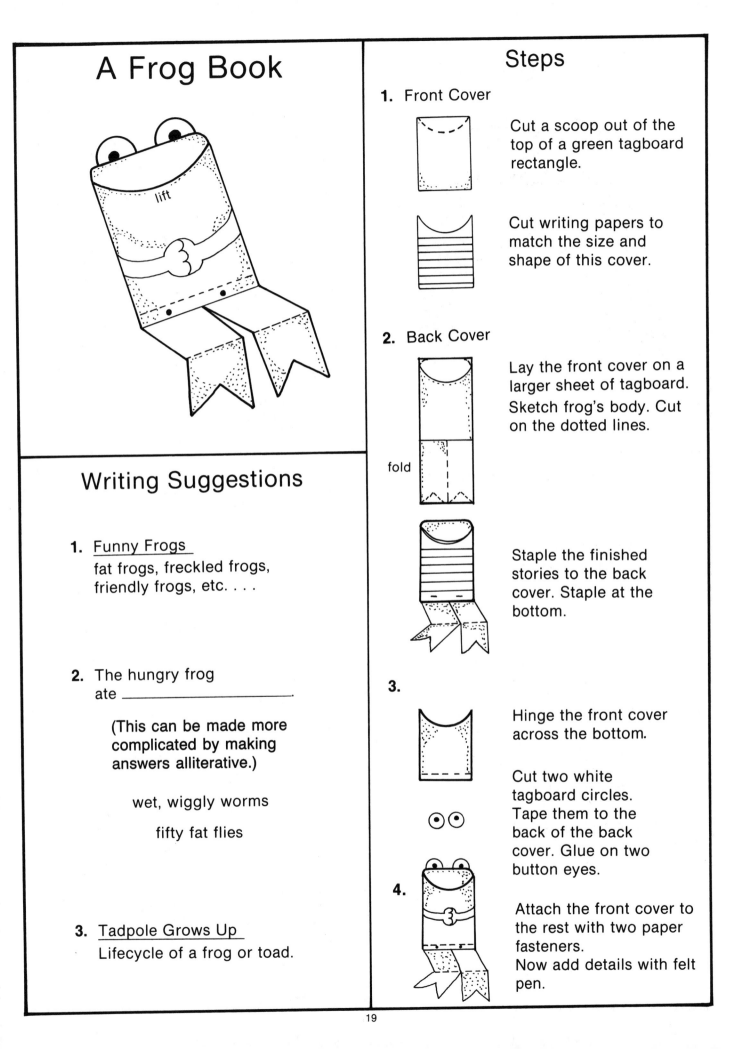

Writing Suggestions

1. <u>Funny Frogs</u>
fat frogs, freckled frogs,
friendly frogs, etc. . . .

2. The hungry frog
ate _____.

(This can be made more
complicated by making
answers alliterative.)

wet, wiggly worms

fifty fat flies

3. <u>Tadpole Grows Up</u>
Lifecycle of a frog or toad.

Steps

1. Front Cover

Cut a scoop out of the
top of a green tagboard
rectangle.

Cut writing papers to
match the size and
shape of this cover.

2. Back Cover

Lay the front cover on a
larger sheet of tagboard.
Sketch frog's body. Cut
on the dotted lines.

Staple the finished
stories to the back
cover. Staple at the
bottom.

3.

Hinge the front cover
across the bottom.

Cut two white
tagboard circles.
Tape them to the
back of the back
cover. Glue on two
button eyes.

4.

Attach the front cover to
the rest with two paper
fasteners.
Now add details with felt
pen.

The Pig Book

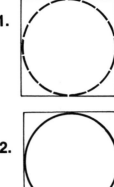

_____ (title) _____

by _____

Writing Suggestions

1. <u>Pigs at Play</u>
How are the pigs having fun? Rolling in the mud, grunting a merry tune...?

2. <u>The Purple Piglet</u>
What happens when the newborn piglet turns out to be bright purple.

3. <u>Pig Poems</u>
These can be as simple as 2 line couplets

> I saw a pig
> begin to dig.

to more complicated verse forms.

4. <u>All About Pigs</u>
Paragraphs of true facts about pigs.

Steps

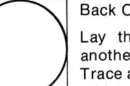

1. Front Cover
Cut a circle for a front cover from pink tagboard. Cut writing paper in this shape.

2. Back Cover
Lay the front cover on another sheet of pink tag. Trace around the circle & add the pig's feet. Cut out.

3. Cut three circles from pink paper. Assemble and paste to front cover.

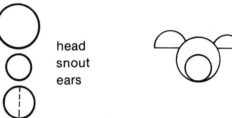

head
snout
ears

Slip a busy red paper tongue under his snout if you like.

Add details with felt pen.

4. Staple the stories to the back cover.

5. Hinge the front cover at top. (See page 4.)

Place the front cover over the stories. Punch two holes and tie it all together with a yarn or ribbon bow.

A Lamb Book

Writing Suggestions

1. <u>Animal Sounds</u>
   "Baa-baa," said the sheep.
   "Cluck-cluck," chirped the hen.

2. Little Bo-Peep found her sheep.

   Where?
   How did she get them home?

3. <u>Strange Sheep</u>
   An unusual flock of sheep were discovered in the mountains.

4. Discuss the process of how wool is made ready for weaving.

   Read *Charlie and His Cloak* by Tomie de Paola.

Steps

1. Front Cover

Cut a cloud shape from a white tagboard square.

Cut writing paper in the same shape.

2. Back Cover

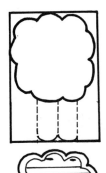

Lay the front cover on a larger sheet of white tagboard.
Sketch around it and add the legs.

Sketch ᘓ on the legs. Color the rest of the legs black.

Staple the finished stories to the back cover. Staple only across the top.

3.

Draw lamb's head. Color it black. Glue on two buttons for eyes. A pink felt nose is a must.

Cut ears from black paper or felt. Glue in place.

Hinge the front cover across the top.

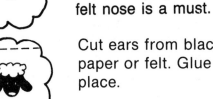

Attach the front cover by punching two holes and tying it all together with a pink ribbon.

The Whale Book

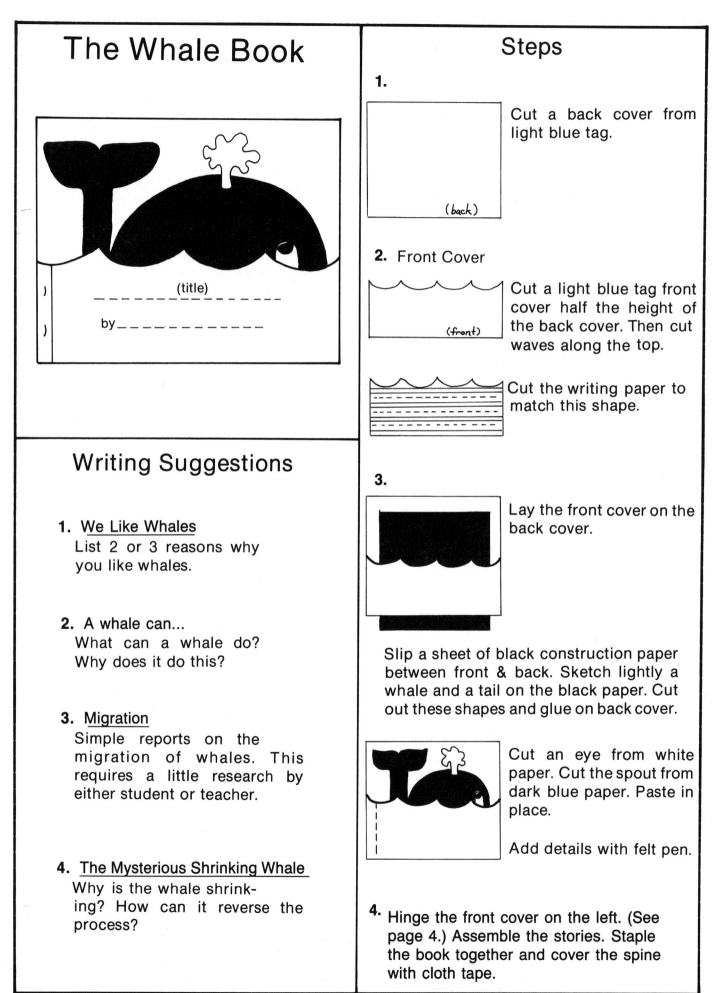

(title) _ _ _ _ _ _ _ _ _ _ _ _ _

by _ _ _ _ _ _ _ _ _ _ _ _ _

Writing Suggestions

1. <u>We Like Whales</u>
List 2 or 3 reasons why you like whales.

2. A whale can...
What can a whale do? Why does it do this?

3. <u>Migration</u>
Simple reports on the migration of whales. This requires a little research by either student or teacher.

4. <u>The Mysterious Shrinking Whale</u>
Why is the whale shrinking? How can it reverse the process?

Steps

1.

(back)

Cut a back cover from light blue tag.

2. Front Cover

(front)

Cut a light blue tag front cover half the height of the back cover. Then cut waves along the top.

Cut the writing paper to match this shape.

3.

Lay the front cover on the back cover.

Slip a sheet of black construction paper between front & back. Sketch lightly a whale and a tail on the black paper. Cut out these shapes and glue on back cover.

Cut an eye from white paper. Cut the spout from dark blue paper. Paste in place.

Add details with felt pen.

4. Hinge the front cover on the left. (See page 4.) Assemble the stories. Staple the book together and cover the spine with cloth tape.

The Crocodile

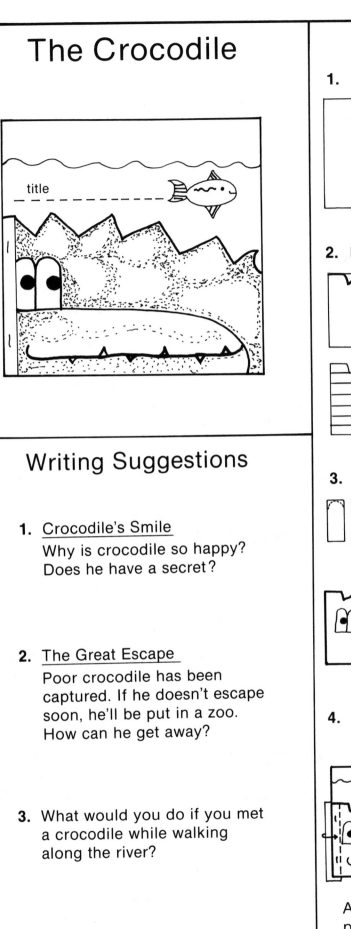

title

Writing Suggestions

1. <u>Crocodile's Smile</u>

Why is crocodile so happy?
Does he have a secret?

2. <u>The Great Escape</u>

Poor crocodile has been
captured. If he doesn't escape
soon, he'll be put in a zoo.
How can he get away?

3. What would you do if you met
a crocodile while walking
along the river?

Steps

1. Back Cover

Cut the back cover from
a blue tag square.

2. Front Cover

Cut a green tag front
cover three quarters the
height of the back cover.
Then cut a zig-zag line
across the top.

Cut writing paper to
match this shape.

3.

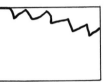

Cut the eyes from white
construction paper.
Paste the eyes on the
green tag (1″ from the
left edge).

Draw all details on the front
cover with felt tip pen.

4. Hinge the front cover on the left. See
page 4 for details.

Assemble the stories.
Staple the book together and
cover the spine with cloth
tape.

Add details to the back cover with felt
pen.

A Groundhog Book

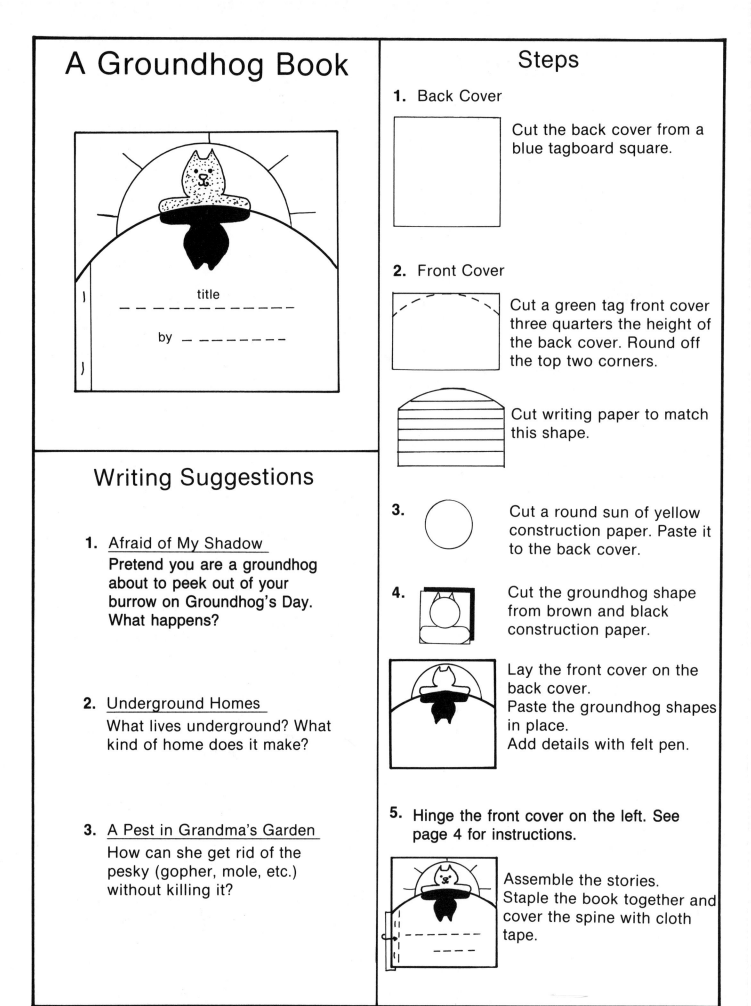

title
- - - - - - - - - - -
by - - - - - - - -

Writing Suggestions

1. Afraid of My Shadow
Pretend you are a groundhog about to peek out of your burrow on Groundhog's Day. What happens?

2. Underground Homes
What lives underground? What kind of home does it make?

3. A Pest in Grandma's Garden
How can she get rid of the pesky (gopher, mole, etc.) without killing it?

Steps

1. Back Cover

Cut the back cover from a blue tagboard square.

2. Front Cover

Cut a green tag front cover three quarters the height of the back cover. Round off the top two corners.

Cut writing paper to match this shape.

3. Cut a round sun of yellow construction paper. Paste it to the back cover.

4. Cut the groundhog shape from brown and black construction paper.

Lay the front cover on the back cover.
Paste the groundhog shapes in place.
Add details with felt pen.

5. Hinge the front cover on the left. See page 4 for instructions.

Assemble the stories. Staple the book together and cover the spine with cloth tape.

The Martian

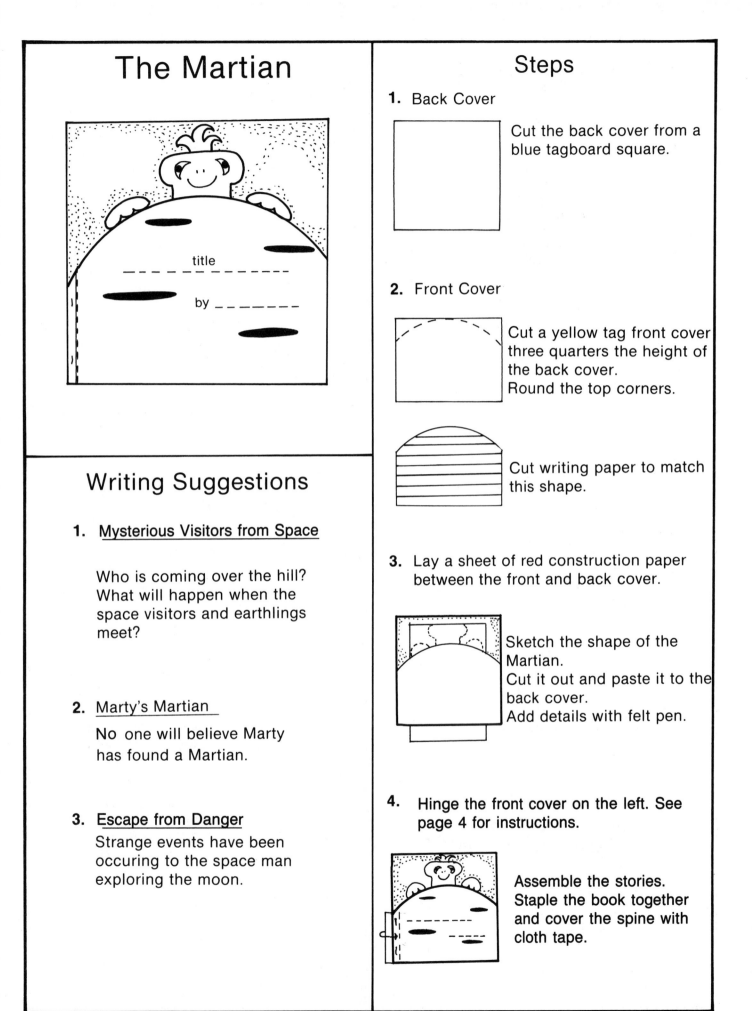

Writing Suggestions

1. Mysterious Visitors from Space

Who is coming over the hill? What will happen when the space visitors and earthlings meet?

2. Marty's Martian

No one will believe Marty has found a Martian.

3. Escape from Danger

Strange events have been occuring to the space man exploring the moon.

Steps

1. Back Cover

Cut the back cover from a blue tagboard square.

2. Front Cover

Cut a yellow tag front cover three quarters the height of the back cover.
Round the top corners.

Cut writing paper to match this shape.

3. Lay a sheet of red construction paper between the front and back cover.

Sketch the shape of the Martian.
Cut it out and paste it to the back cover.
Add details with felt pen.

4. Hinge the front cover on the left. See page 4 for instructions.

Assemble the stories.
Staple the book together and cover the spine with cloth tape.

A Bat Book

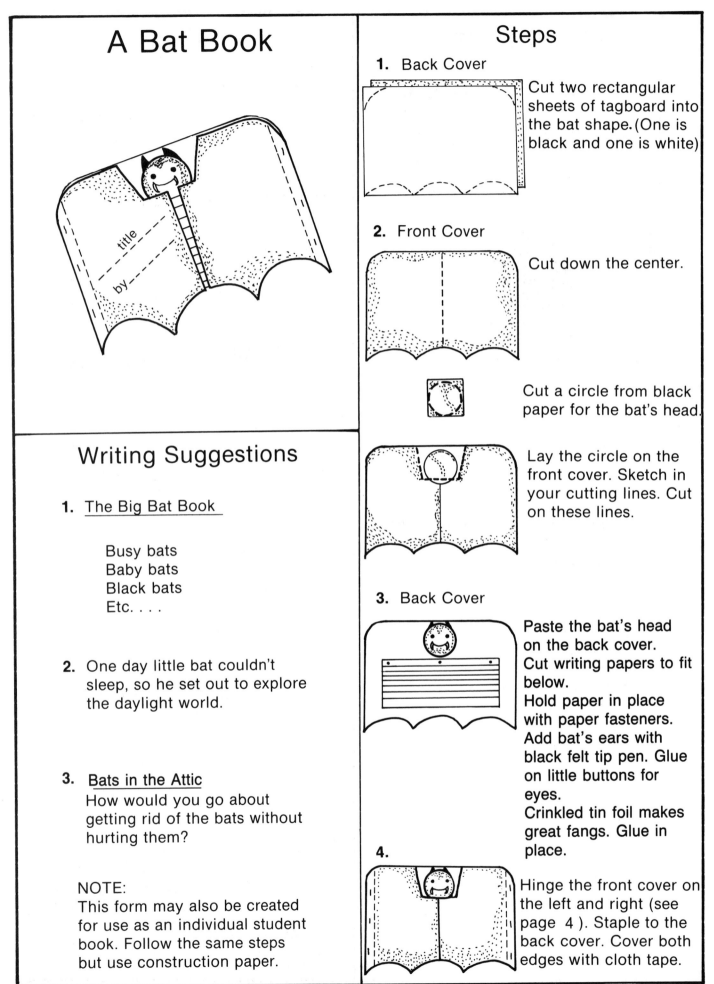

title ___
by ___

Writing Suggestions

1. The Big Bat Book

Busy bats
Baby bats
Black bats
Etc. . . .

2. One day little bat couldn't sleep, so he set out to explore the daylight world.

3. Bats in the Attic
How would you go about getting rid of the bats without hurting them?

NOTE:
This form may also be created for use as an individual student book. Follow the same steps but use construction paper.

Steps

1. Back Cover

Cut two rectangular sheets of tagboard into the bat shape. (One is black and one is white)

2. Front Cover

Cut down the center.

Cut a circle from black paper for the bat's head.

Lay the circle on the front cover. Sketch in your cutting lines. Cut on these lines.

3. Back Cover

Paste the bat's head on the back cover.
Cut writing papers to fit below.
Hold paper in place with paper fasteners.
Add bat's ears with black felt tip pen. Glue on little buttons for eyes.
Crinkled tin foil makes great fangs. Glue in place.

4.

Hinge the front cover on the left and right (see page 4). Staple to the back cover. Cover both edges with cloth tape.

The Castle

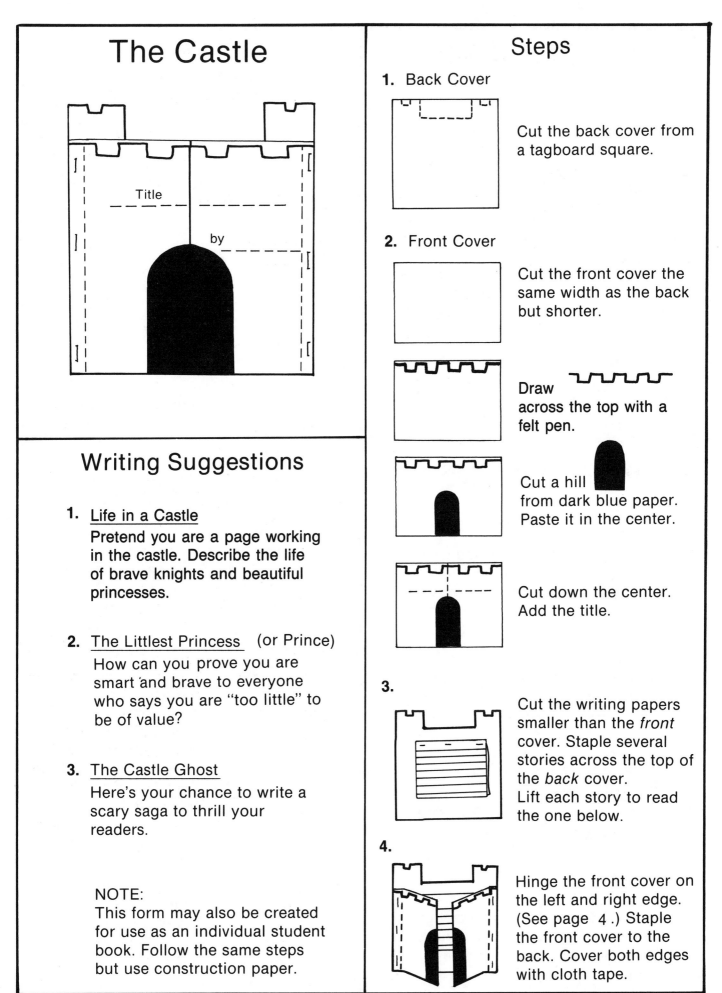

Writing Suggestions

1. <u>Life in a Castle</u>
Pretend you are a page working in the castle. Describe the life of brave knights and beautiful princesses.

2. <u>The Littlest Princess</u> (or Prince)
How can you prove you are smart and brave to everyone who says you are "too little" to be of value?

3. <u>The Castle Ghost</u>
Here's your chance to write a scary saga to thrill your readers.

NOTE:
This form may also be created for use as an individual student book. Follow the same steps but use construction paper.

Steps

1. Back Cover

Cut the back cover from a tagboard square.

2. Front Cover

Cut the front cover the same width as the back but shorter.

Draw across the top with a felt pen.

Cut a hill from dark blue paper. Paste it in the center.

Cut down the center. Add the title.

3.

Cut the writing papers smaller than the *front* cover. Staple several stories across the top of the *back* cover.
Lift each story to read the one below.

4.

Hinge the front cover on the left and right edge. (See page 4.) Staple the front cover to the back. Cover both edges with cloth tape.

An OPEN House

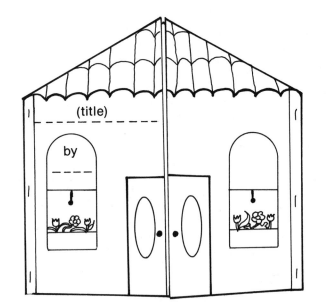

(title)

by

Steps

1.

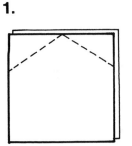

Cut two squares of colorful tagboard into the basic house shape.

2. Front Cover

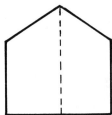

Cut down the center.

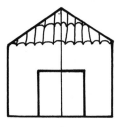

Use a felt pen to make a roof.
Cut a door from a contrasting color construction paper.
Paste it in the center.

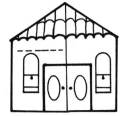

Cut two windows from white paper. Paste them on each side of the door. Add details with a felt pen. Print the title.

3. Back Cover

Cut the story papers smaller than the cover. Staple several stories across the top of the back cover.
Lift each story to read the one below.

4.

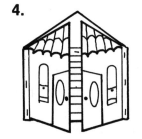

Hinge the front cover on the left and the right edge. (See page 4.)
Staple the front cover to the back. Cover both edges with cloth tape.

Writing Suggestions

1. _____'s House
Describe your own home. Make the description so clear that a stranger would recognize it from your words.

2. Moving In
A new family has come to live next door.

3. The Mysterious House
Strange sounds and sights have been seen in this strange house.

NOTE:
This form may also be created for use as an individual student book. Follow the same steps but use construction paper.

A Cloud

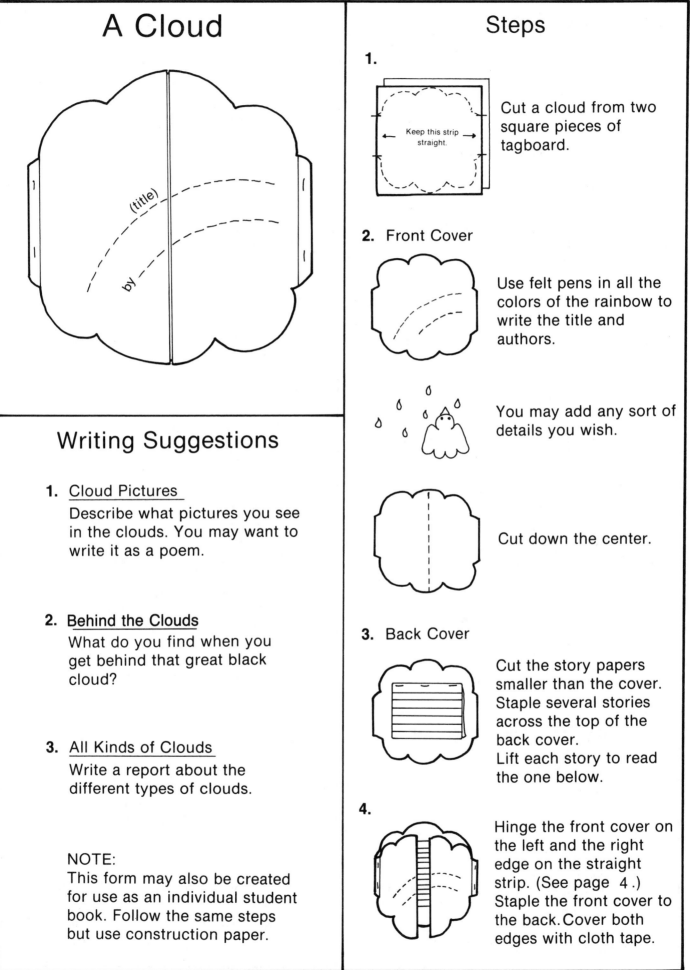

(title)

by

Writing Suggestions

1. <u>Cloud Pictures</u>
Describe what pictures you see in the clouds. You may want to write it as a poem.

2. <u>**Behind the Clouds**</u>
What do you find when you get behind that great black cloud?

3. <u>All Kinds of Clouds</u>
Write a report about the different types of clouds.

NOTE:
This form may also be created for use as an individual student book. Follow the same steps but use construction paper.

Steps

1.

Keep this strip straight.

Cut a cloud from two square pieces of tagboard.

2. Front Cover

Use felt pens in all the colors of the rainbow to write the title and authors.

You may add any sort of details you wish.

Cut down the center.

3. Back Cover

Cut the story papers smaller than the cover. Staple several stories across the top of the back cover.
Lift each story to read the one below.

4.

Hinge the front cover on the left and the right edge on the straight strip. (See page 4.) Staple the front cover to the back. Cover both edges with cloth tape.

Chocolate Chip Cookie

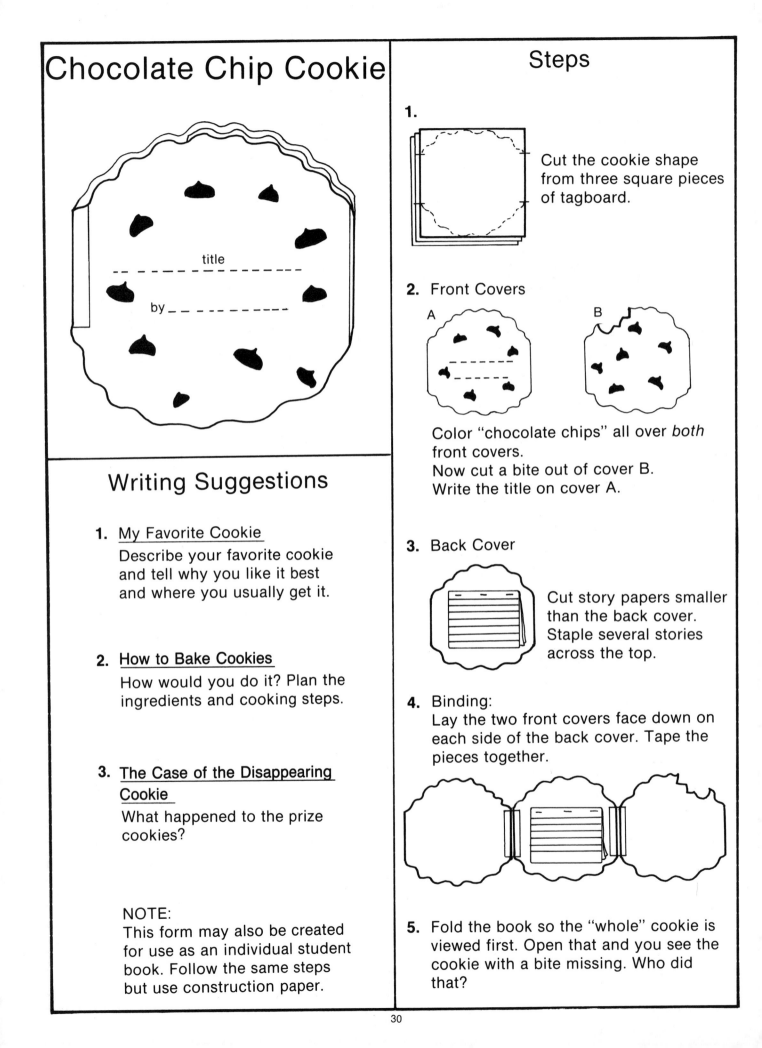

title _ _ _ _ _ _ _ _ _ _ _ _ _ _

by _ _ _ _ _ _ _ _ _ _ _ _

Writing Suggestions

1. <u>My Favorite Cookie</u>
   Describe your favorite cookie and tell why you like it best and where you usually get it.

2. <u>How to Bake Cookies</u>
   How would you do it? Plan the ingredients and cooking steps.

3. <u>The Case of the Disappearing Cookie</u>
   What happened to the prize cookies?

NOTE:
This form may also be created for use as an individual student book. Follow the same steps but use construction paper.

Steps

1. Cut the cookie shape from three square pieces of tagboard.

2. Front Covers

   A   B

   Color "chocolate chips" all over *both* front covers.
   Now cut a bite out of cover B.
   Write the title on cover A.

3. Back Cover

   Cut story papers smaller than the back cover. Staple several stories across the top.

4. Binding:
   Lay the two front covers face down on each side of the back cover. Tape the pieces together.

5. Fold the book so the "whole" cookie is viewed first. Open that and you see the cookie with a bite missing. Who did that?

A Cave

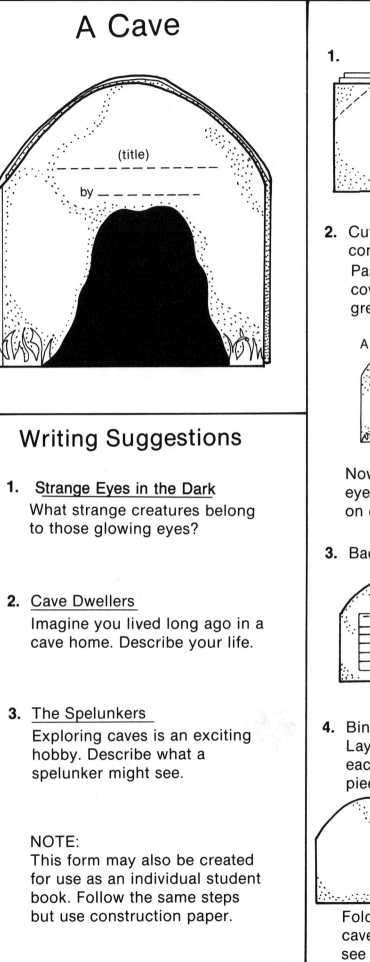

(title)

by _____

Writing Suggestions

1. <u>Strange Eyes in the Dark</u>
What strange creatures belong to those glowing eyes?

2. <u>Cave Dwellers</u>
Imagine you lived long ago in a cave home. Describe your life.

3. <u>The Spelunkers</u>
Exploring caves is an exciting hobby. Describe what a spelunker might see.

NOTE:
This form may also be created for use as an individual student book. Follow the same steps but use construction paper.

Steps

1.

Cut the cave shape from three square brown pieces of tagboard.

2. Cut two cave openings from black construction paper.
Paste them on the brown covers. Add scraps of green paper as grass.

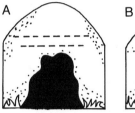

A   B

Now cut out two mysterious yellow eyes to paste on cover B. Write the title on cover A.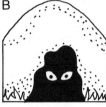

3. Back cover

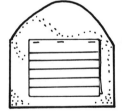

Cut story papers smaller than the back cover. Staple several stories across the top.

4. Binding:
Lay the two front covers face down on each side of the back cover. Tape the pieces together.

Fold the book so you see the black cave first. Then you open it and you see the eyes. Who do they belong to?

ACCORDION BOOKS

Accordion books are best used for small group or individual books. Too many pages are difficult to work with. Poetry, descriptive paragraphs, life cycles, and steps in making something are all suitable writing ideas for accordion books.

Accordion books can also be used to display students' work if made from tag or cardboard so they can be set up open on a table or shelf.

In making accordion books, it is especially important to read directions carefully and to practice folding the paper before you try doing them with children. The best results come when you feel comfortable about the steps involved.

Writing suggestions are provided for each accordian book idea. Also, pattern forms are provided for covers where needed.

Accordion books can be made from:

> Folded butcher paper
> Tag for covers, butcher paper inside
> All tag

● Mini-accordion Book

> This accordion book is a good one for practice. It shows that an accordion book can be made any size. Begin with a strip of 6" x 18" construction paper folded into quarters. Tape 4½" x 6" pieces of tag to the front and back to create a cover. Now write!

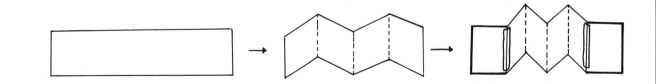

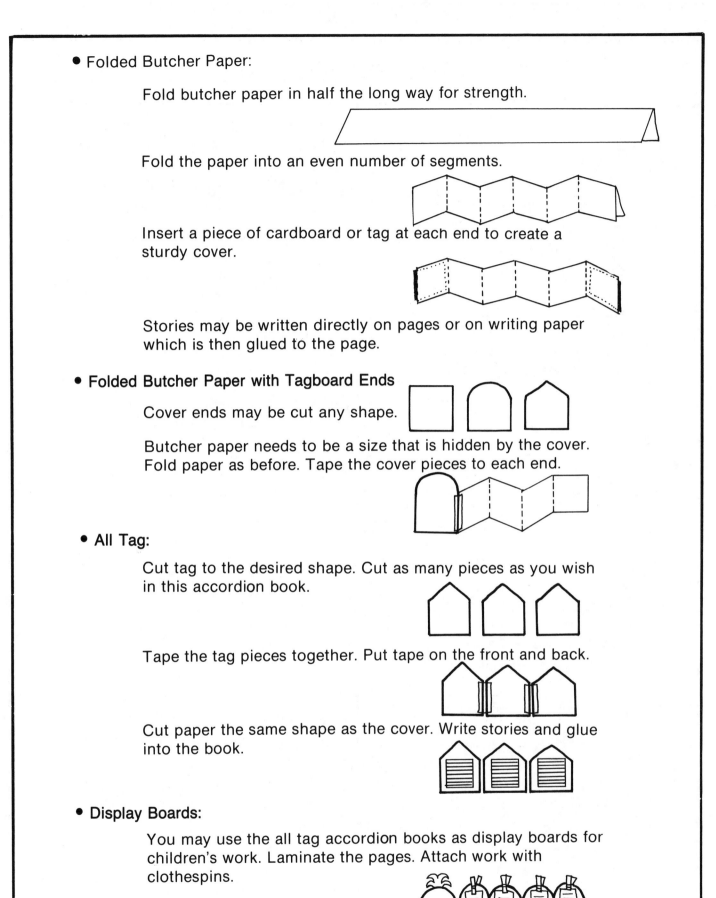

- **Folded Butcher Paper:**

    Fold butcher paper in half the long way for strength.

    Fold the paper into an even number of segments.

    Insert a piece of cardboard or tag at each end to create a sturdy cover.

    Stories may be written directly on pages or on writing paper which is then glued to the page.

- **Folded Butcher Paper with Tagboard Ends**

    Cover ends may be cut any shape.

    Butcher paper needs to be a size that is hidden by the cover. Fold paper as before. Tape the cover pieces to each end.

- **All Tag:**

    Cut tag to the desired shape. Cut as many pieces as you wish in this accordion book.

    Tape the tag pieces together. Put tape on the front and back.

    Cut paper the same shape as the cover. Write stories and glue into the book.

- **Display Boards:**

    You may use the all tag accordion books as display boards for children's work. Laminate the pages. Attach work with clothespins.

    You may wish to create a more elaborate accordion book to use as your display board.

Accordion Books

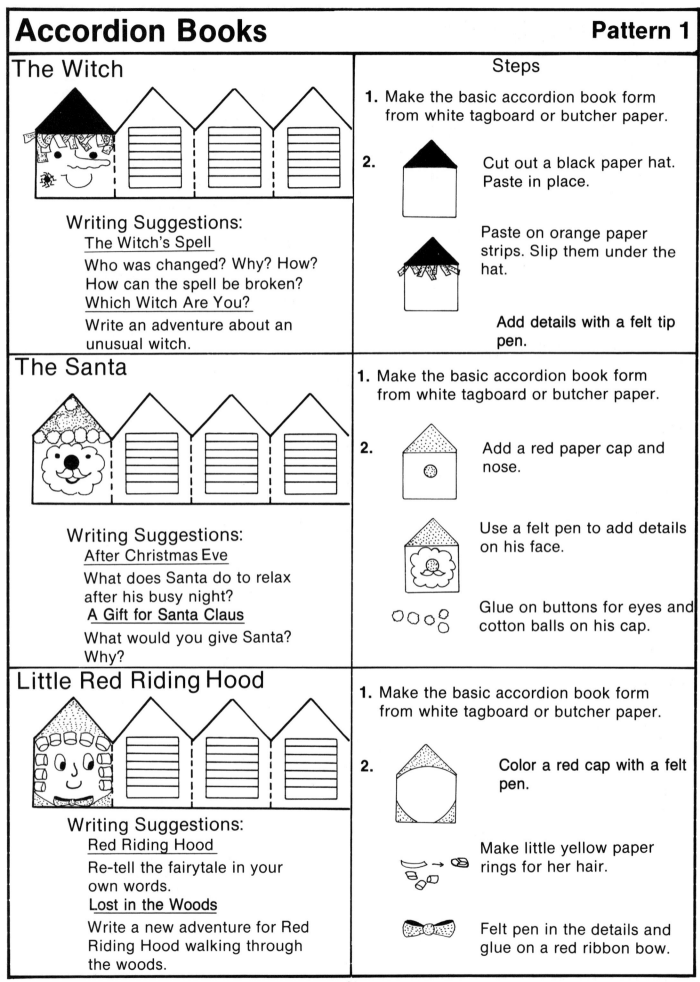

The Witch

Writing Suggestions:

The Witch's Spell

Who was changed? Why? How? How can the spell be broken?

Which Witch Are You?

Write an adventure about an unusual witch.

Steps

1. Make the basic accordion book form from white tagboard or butcher paper.

2. Cut out a black paper hat. Paste in place.

Paste on orange paper strips. Slip them under the hat.

Add details with a felt tip pen.

The Santa

Writing Suggestions:

After Christmas Eve

What does Santa do to relax after his busy night?

A Gift for Santa Claus

What would you give Santa? Why?

1. Make the basic accordion book form from white tagboard or butcher paper.

2. Add a red paper cap and nose.

Use a felt pen to add details on his face.

Glue on buttons for eyes and cotton balls on his cap.

Little Red Riding Hood

Writing Suggestions:

Red Riding Hood

Re-tell the fairytale in your own words.

Lost in the Woods

Write a new adventure for Red Riding Hood walking through the woods.

1. Make the basic accordion book form from white tagboard or butcher paper.

2. Color a red cap with a felt pen.

Make little yellow paper rings for her hair.

Felt pen in the details and glue on a red ribbon bow.

Accordion Books

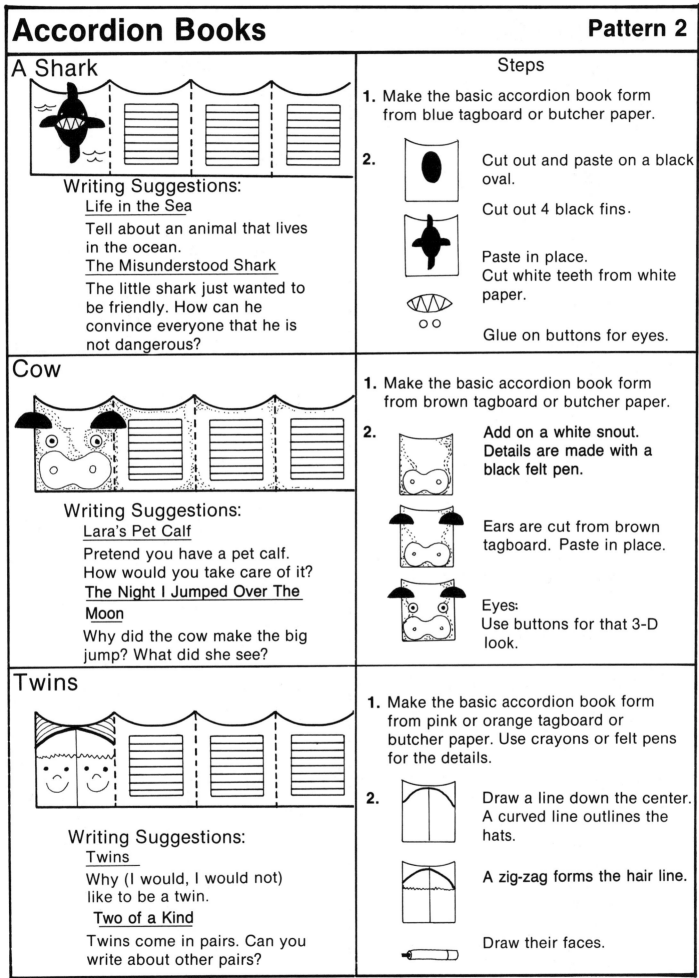

A Shark

Writing Suggestions:

Life in the Sea

Tell about an animal that lives in the ocean.

The Misunderstood Shark

The little shark just wanted to be friendly. How can he convince everyone that he is not dangerous?

Steps

1. Make the basic accordion book form from blue tagboard or butcher paper.

2. Cut out and paste on a black oval.

Cut out 4 black fins.

Paste in place.
Cut white teeth from white paper.

Glue on buttons for eyes.

Cow

Writing Suggestions:

Lara's Pet Calf

Pretend you have a pet calf. How would you take care of it?

The Night I Jumped Over The Moon

Why did the cow make the big jump? What did she see?

1. Make the basic accordion book form from brown tagboard or butcher paper.

2. Add on a white snout. Details are made with a black felt pen.

Ears are cut from brown tagboard. Paste in place.

Eyes:
Use buttons for that 3-D look.

Twins

Writing Suggestions:

Twins

Why (I would, I would not) like to be a twin.

Two of a Kind

Twins come in pairs. Can you write about other pairs?

1. Make the basic accordion book form from pink or orange tagboard or butcher paper. Use crayons or felt pens for the details.

2. Draw a line down the center. A curved line outlines the hats.

A zig-zag forms the hair line.

Draw their faces.

Accordion Books **Pattern 3**

The Eagle

Steps

1. Make the basic accordion book form from white tagboard or butcher paper.

2. Draw the eyes with felt pen.

   Cut an orange beak from tag. Tape a paper clip to the inside. Paste only the top of the beak to the cover. Add black feathers at the neck with felt pen.

   Tuck a note in his beak (under the paper clip).

Writing Suggestions:

Eagle Express

What important message is eagle carrying? From whom? To whom?

American Eagle

Why do you think the eagle is one symbol of the U.S.A.?

Eskimo & Igloo

Writing Suggestions:

Life in an Igloo

Describe what you think it would be like living in an igloo.

Arctic Adventure

This Eskimo is about to go hunting. What do you think will happen?

1. Make the basic accordion book form from white tagboard or butcher paper. Use crayons to add the details.

2. Draw the Eskimo.

   Outline the ice blocks with blue.

Mirror Mirror on the Wall

Writing Suggestions:

Mirror, Mirror on the Wall

What question would you ask the mirror? What would it answer?

The Magic Mirror

What do you see when you look in the magic mirror?

1. Make the basic accordion book form from white tagboard or butcher paper.

2. Cut tin foil to fit inside this shape. Tape it around the outside with a cloth tape.

   Use a permanent marker to print the title on the tin foil.

Accordion Books

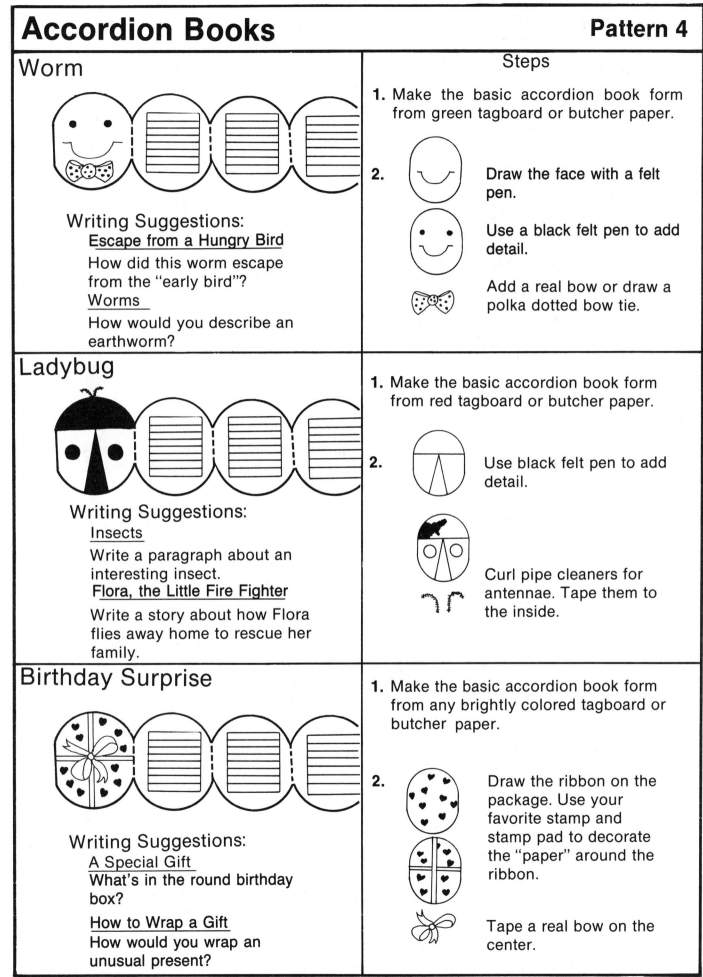

Worm

Writing Suggestions:

Escape from a Hungry Bird

How did this worm escape from the "early bird"?

Worms

How would you describe an earthworm?

Steps

1. Make the basic accordion book form from green tagboard or butcher paper.

2. Draw the face with a felt pen.

Use a black felt pen to add detail.

Add a real bow or draw a polka dotted bow tie.

Ladybug

Writing Suggestions:

Insects

Write a paragraph about an interesting insect.

Flora, the Little Fire Fighter

Write a story about how Flora flies away home to rescue her family.

1. Make the basic accordion book form from red tagboard or butcher paper.

2. Use black felt pen to add detail.

Curl pipe cleaners for antennae. Tape them to the inside.

Birthday Surprise

Writing Suggestions:

A Special Gift

What's in the round birthday box?

How to Wrap a Gift

How would you wrap an unusual present?

1. Make the basic accordion book form from any brightly colored tagboard or butcher paper.

2. Draw the ribbon on the package. Use your favorite stamp and stamp pad to decorate the "paper" around the ribbon.

Tape a real bow on the center.

FLAP BOOKS

Flap illustrations are a great motivation because of the "surprise" or "mystery" element.

Each idea for flap pages includes writing suggestions. These ideas can be used as illustrations for group books or as one of a series of illustrations for an individual story. The best individual books revolve around a "search." Looking for lost homework, a missing pet, a birthday surprise, etc. can involve a wide variety of flaps as the search progresses.

Before beginning the project, read all directions carefully. The flaps need to be made from construction paper for strength. Size and shape will depend on the story situation.

Simple Flaps: **Squares and rectangles can become doors, lunch boxes, gifts, etc. Simply cut the shape the size you wish, draw a picture on it, fold an edge, add some paste, and you are all set!**

Special Flaps: Shapes can be cut to fit your story. Cut, fold edge, and paste.

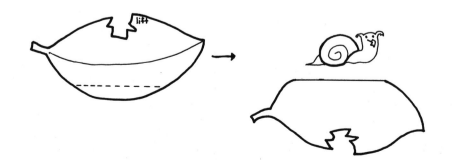

The Mystery Door

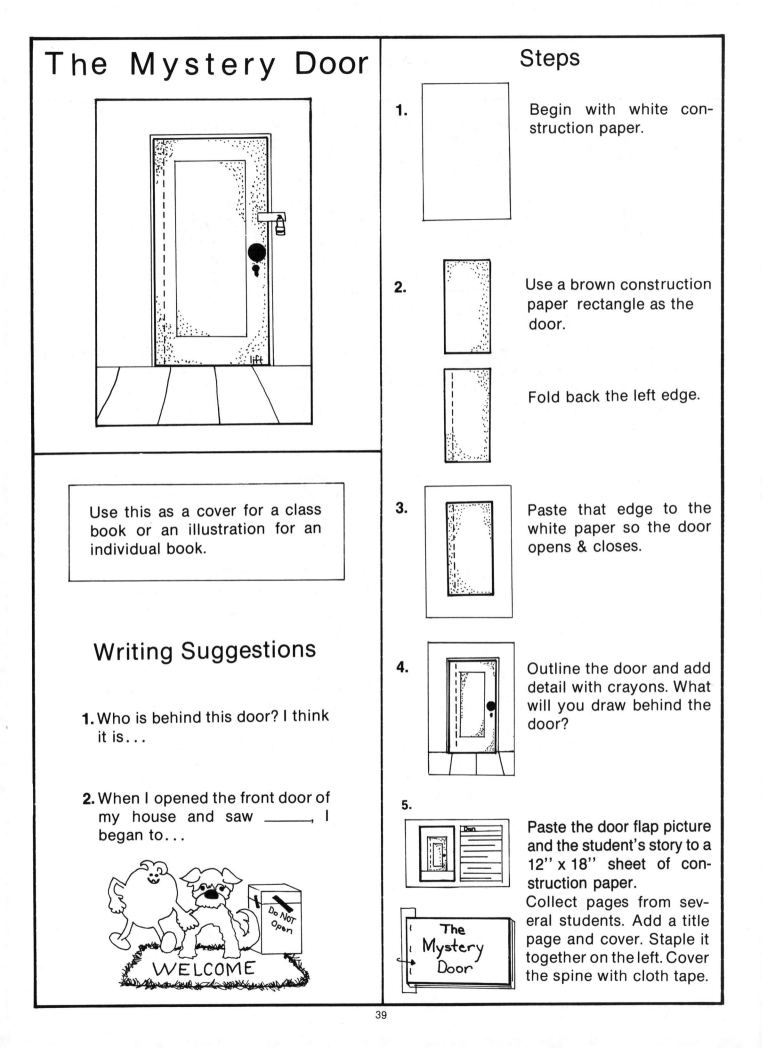

Use this as a cover for a class book or an illustration for an individual book.

Writing Suggestions

1. Who is behind this door? I think it is...

2. When I opened the front door of my house and saw _____, I began to...

WELCOME

Steps

1. Begin with white construction paper.

2. Use a brown construction paper rectangle as the door.

Fold back the left edge.

3. Paste that edge to the white paper so the door opens & closes.

4. Outline the door and add detail with crayons. What will you draw behind the door?

5. Paste the door flap picture and the student's story to a 12'' x 18'' sheet of construction paper.
Collect pages from several students. Add a title page and cover. Staple it together on the left. Cover the spine with cloth tape.

Inside the Tent

Writing Suggestions

1. <u>Life in a Tent</u>
Pretend you are a desert nomad living in a tent. What would your life be like?

2. **Sounds in the Night**
Lara and Willie were sleeping in their tent in the backyard when suddenly . . .

3. What would you do if you found a _____ in your tent?

        bear
        skunk
        snake

Steps

1. Begin with black construction paper for the background.

2. 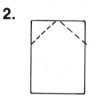 Use brown construction paper for the tent. Cut the top to a peak.

The tent door flap is also brown. Fold back the top edge.

3. Paste the tent and the top edge of the door flap to the black paper.

 **Add details with crayons.**

Use yellow for the moon and tent windows.
Use black for tent poles.
Outline the tent with black.
Lift the door flap and draw who is inside the tent.

4.  Paste the tent picture and student's story to a 12″ x 18″ sheet of construction paper.

5. 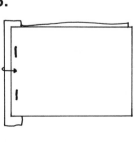 Collect pages from several students.
Add a cover and title page. Staple it together on the left.
Cover the spine with cloth tape.

Under the Bed

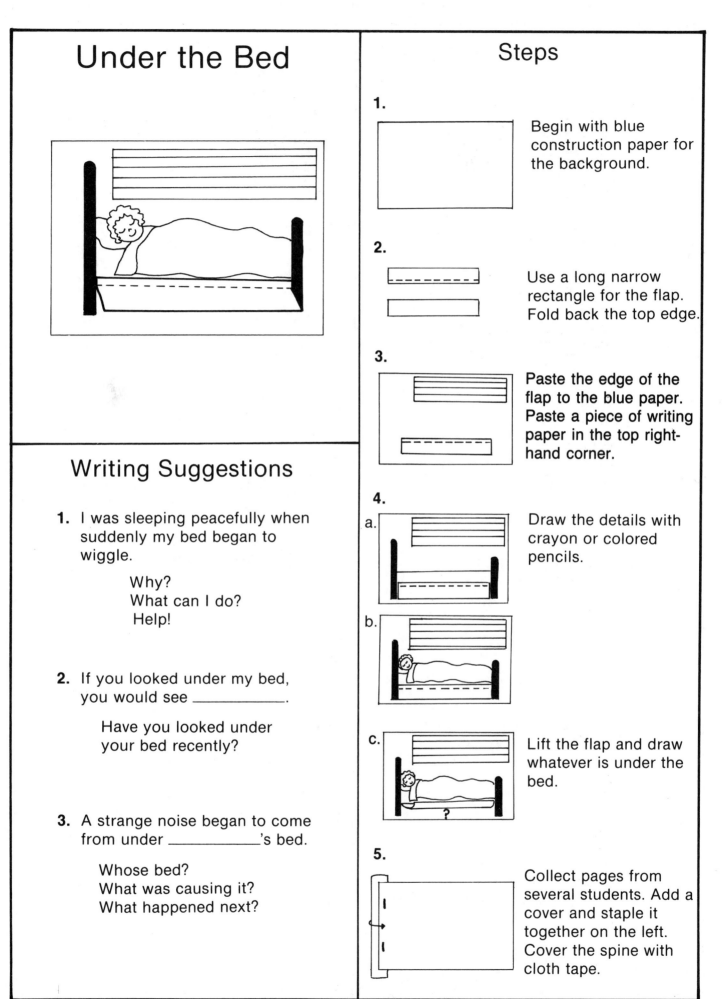

Writing Suggestions

1. I was sleeping peacefully when suddenly my bed began to wiggle.

> Why?
> What can I do?
> Help!

2. If you looked under my bed, you would see _____.

> Have you looked under your bed recently?

3. A strange noise began to come from under _____'s bed.

> Whose bed?
> What was causing it?
> What happened next?

Steps

1. Begin with blue construction paper for the background.

2. Use a long narrow rectangle for the flap. Fold back the top edge.

3. Paste the edge of the flap to the blue paper. Paste a piece of writing paper in the top right-hand corner.

4.
a. Draw the details with crayon or colored pencils.

b.

c. Lift the flap and draw whatever is under the bed.

5. Collect pages from several students. Add a cover and staple it together on the left. Cover the spine with cloth tape.

Behind the Cupboard Doors

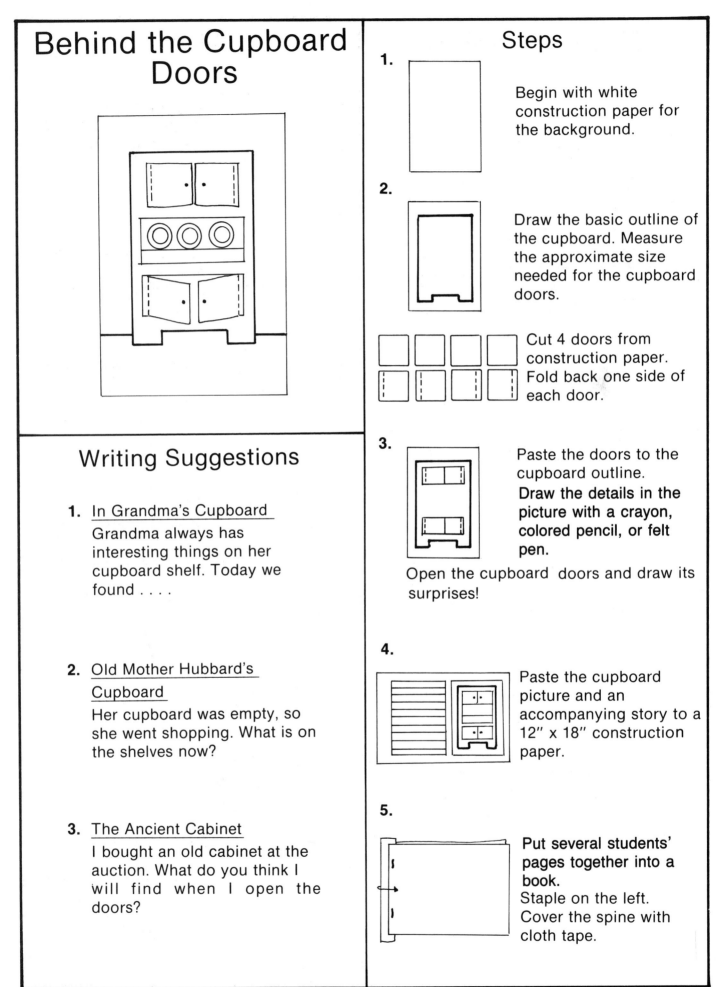

Writing Suggestions

1. <u>In Grandma's Cupboard</u>
Grandma always has interesting things on her cupboard shelf. Today we found . . . .

2. <u>Old Mother Hubbard's Cupboard</u>
Her cupboard was empty, so she went shopping. What is on the shelves now?

3. <u>The Ancient Cabinet</u>
I bought an old cabinet at the auction. What do you think I will find when I open the doors?

Steps

1.
Begin with white construction paper for the background.

2.
Draw the basic outline of the cupboard. Measure the approximate size needed for the cupboard doors.

Cut 4 doors from construction paper. Fold back one side of each door.

3.
Paste the doors to the cupboard outline. **Draw the details in the picture with a crayon, colored pencil, or felt pen.**

Open the cupboard doors and draw its surprises!

4.
Paste the cupboard picture and an accompanying story to a 12" x 18" construction paper.

5.
Put several students' pages together into a book.
Staple on the left. Cover the spine with cloth tape.

The Lunch Box

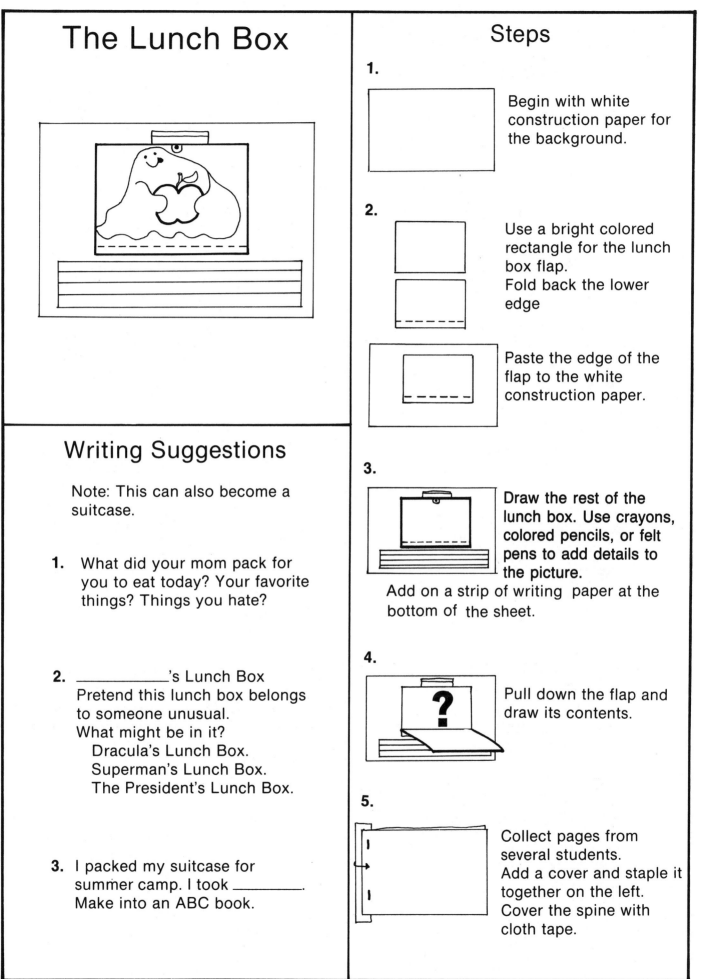

Writing Suggestions

Note: This can also become a suitcase.

1. What did your mom pack for you to eat today? Your favorite things? Things you hate?

2. _____'s Lunch Box
   Pretend this lunch box belongs to someone unusual.
   What might be in it?
   Dracula's Lunch Box.
   Superman's Lunch Box.
   The President's Lunch Box.

3. I packed my suitcase for summer camp. I took _____.
   Make into an ABC book.

Steps

1. Begin with white construction paper for the background.

2. Use a bright colored rectangle for the lunch box flap.
   Fold back the lower edge

   Paste the edge of the flap to the white construction paper.

3. **Draw the rest of the lunch box. Use crayons, colored pencils, or felt pens to add details to the picture.**
   Add on a strip of writing paper at the bottom of the sheet.

4. Pull down the flap and draw its contents.

5. Collect pages from several students.
   Add a cover and staple it together on the left.
   Cover the spine with cloth tape.

What's under the Hood?

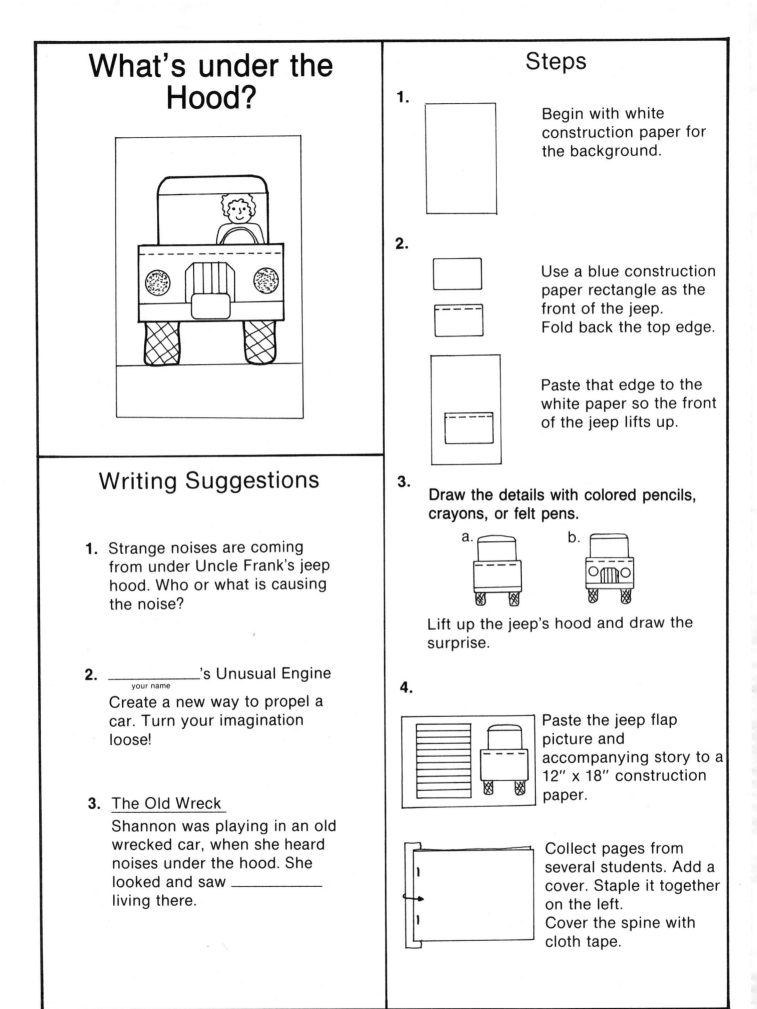

Writing Suggestions

1. Strange noises are coming from under Uncle Frank's jeep hood. Who or what is causing the noise?

2. _____'s Unusual Engine
your name
Create a new way to propel a car. Turn your imagination loose!

3. The Old Wreck
Shannon was playing in an old wrecked car, when she heard noises under the hood. She looked and saw _____ living there.

Steps

1. Begin with white construction paper for the background.

2. Use a blue construction paper rectangle as the front of the jeep.
Fold back the top edge.

Paste that edge to the white paper so the front of the jeep lifts up.

3. Draw the details with colored pencils, crayons, or felt pens.

a.   b.

Lift up the jeep's hood and draw the surprise.

4. Paste the jeep flap picture and accompanying story to a 12" x 18" construction paper.

Collect pages from several students. Add a cover. Staple it together on the left.
Cover the spine with cloth tape.

What's in the Pocket?

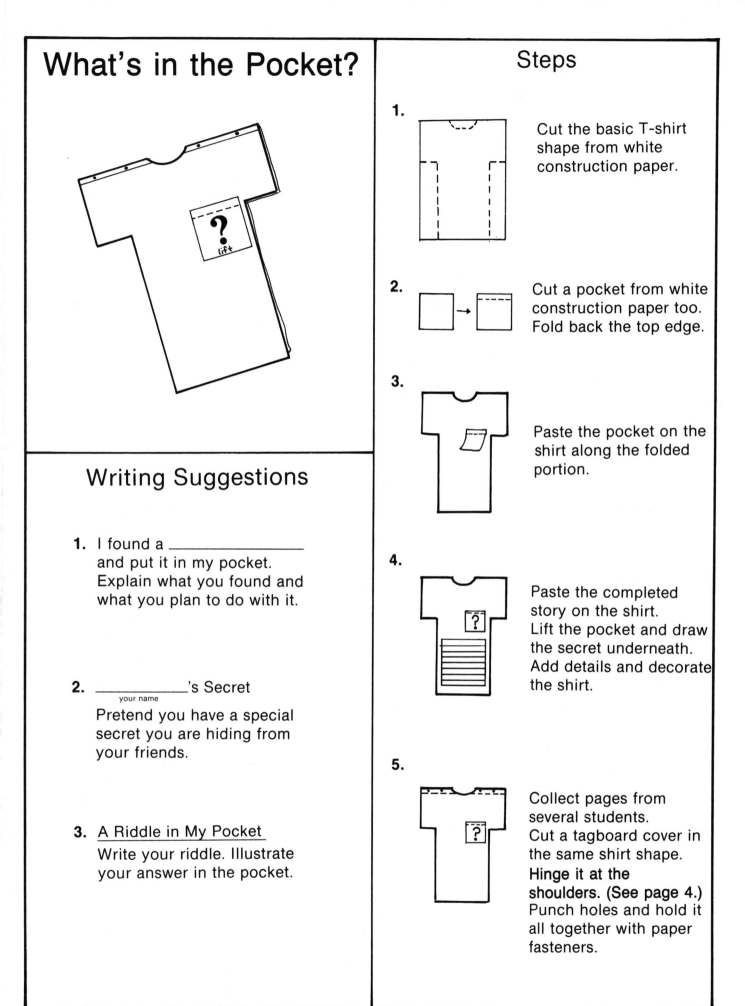

Writing Suggestions

1. I found a _____
and put it in my pocket.
Explain what you found and
what you plan to do with it.

2. _____'s Secret
your name

Pretend you have a special
secret you are hiding from
your friends.

3. <u>A Riddle in My Pocket</u>
Write your riddle. Illustrate
your answer in the pocket.

Steps

1. Cut the basic T-shirt shape from white construction paper.

2. Cut a pocket from white construction paper too. Fold back the top edge.

3. Paste the pocket on the shirt along the folded portion.

4. Paste the completed story on the shirt.
Lift the pocket and draw the secret underneath.
Add details and decorate the shirt.

5. Collect pages from several students.
Cut a tagboard cover in the same shirt shape.
Hinge it at the shoulders. (See page 4.)
Punch holes and hold it all together with paper fasteners.

Keep it under Your Wing

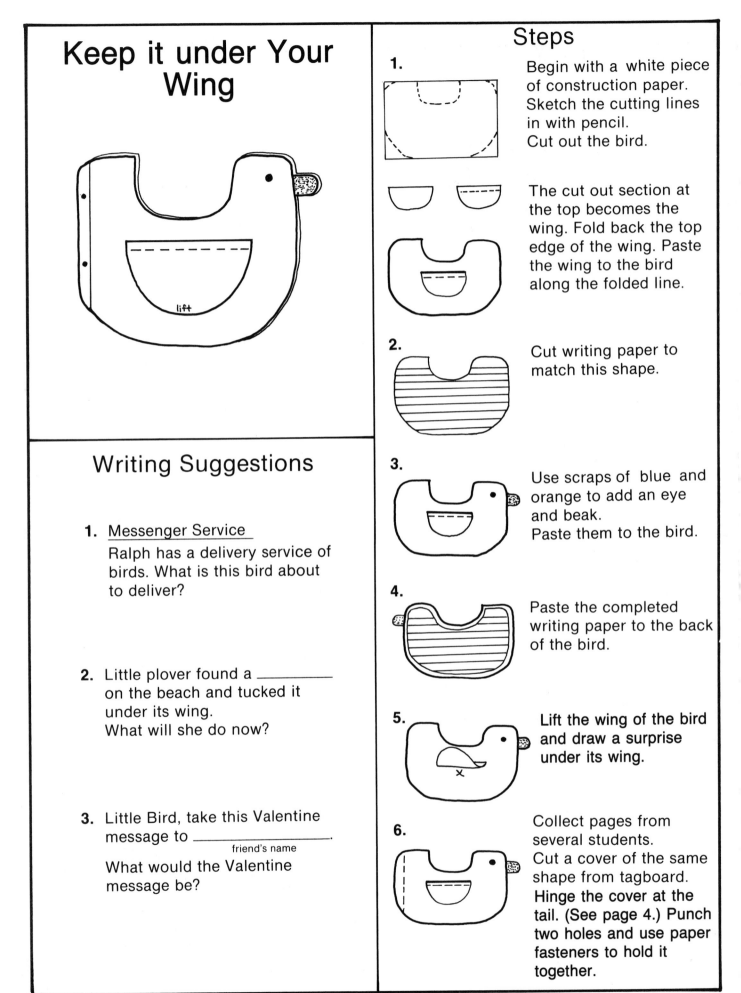

Writing Suggestions

1. <u>Messenger Service</u>

Ralph has a delivery service of birds. What is this bird about to deliver?

2. Little plover found a _____ on the beach and tucked it under its wing.
What will she do now?

3. Little Bird, take this Valentine message to _____.
friend's name
What would the Valentine message be?

Steps

1. Begin with a white piece of construction paper.
Sketch the cutting lines in with pencil.
Cut out the bird.

The cut out section at the top becomes the wing. Fold back the top edge of the wing. Paste the wing to the bird along the folded line.

2. Cut writing paper to match this shape.

3. Use scraps of blue and orange to add an eye and beak.
Paste them to the bird.

4. Paste the completed writing paper to the back of the bird.

5. Lift the wing of the bird and draw a surprise under its wing.

6. Collect pages from several students.
Cut a cover of the same shape from tagboard.
Hinge the cover at the tail. (See page 4.) Punch two holes and use paper fasteners to hold it together.

Dog with Brown Bag

Writing Suggestions

1. <u>The Doggy Bag</u>

I had too much on my plate at the restaurant, so I brought

_____

home in my "doggy" bag.

2. I packed a picnic lunch for my dog _____. I put in . . . .
dog's name

3. <u>Brown Bag Riddles</u>

Write a "doggy" riddle on the bag. Illustrate the answer under the flap.

Steps

1.

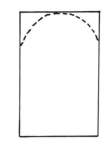

Begin with a sheet of white construction paper. Round off the top corners before you give it to students. Consistency is important.

2.

Draw the basic dog shape.
Children can follow step by step if the teacher demonstrates on the overhead projector.
Invite children to color their dog any color they choose.

a

b

3.

Paste the top of a real flat brown bag just below the dog's mouth.

Lift the bag up and draw the surprise underneath. Paste the story or riddle to the top of the bag.

4.

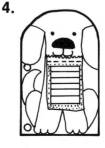

Collect pages from several students. Add a cover cut in the same dog shape.
Punch two holes and hold it all together with two binder rings.

Bear with a Flap

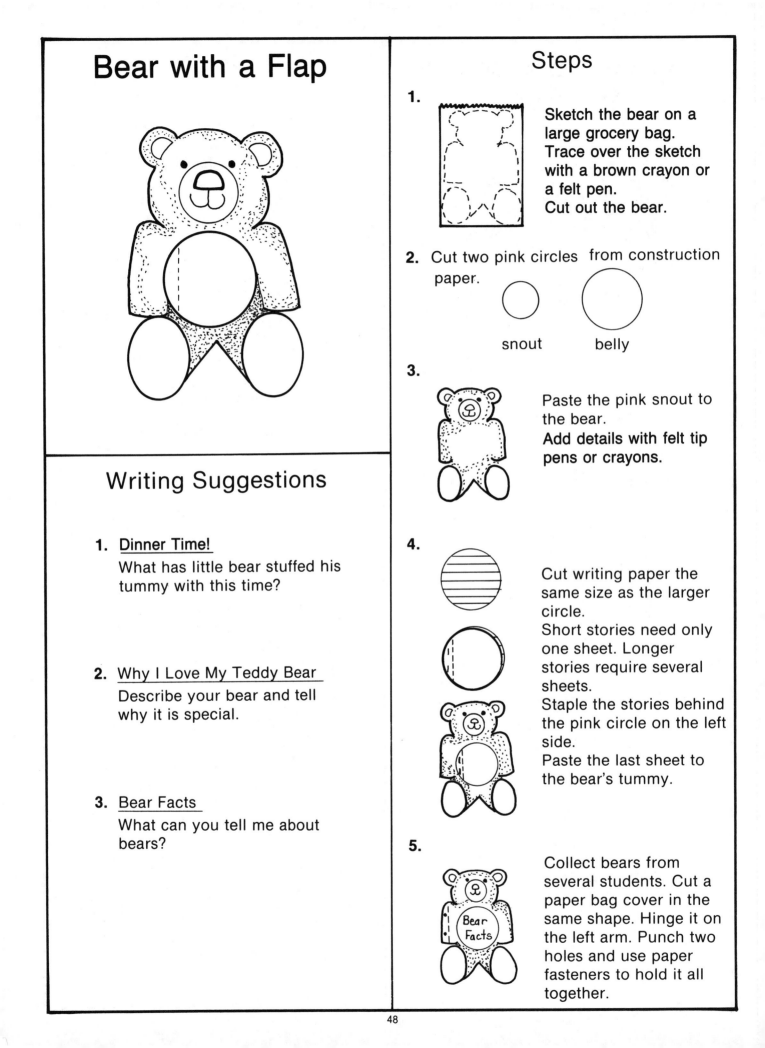

Writing Suggestions

1. <u>Dinner Time!</u>
What has little bear stuffed his tummy with this time?

2. <u>Why I Love My Teddy Bear</u>
Describe your bear and tell why it is special.

3. <u>Bear Facts</u>
What can you tell me about bears?

Steps

1. Sketch the bear on a large grocery bag.
Trace over the sketch with a brown crayon or a felt pen.
Cut out the bear.

2. Cut two pink circles from construction paper.

snout   belly

3. Paste the pink snout to the bear.
Add details with felt tip pens or crayons.

4. Cut writing paper the same size as the larger circle.
Short stories need only one sheet. Longer stories require several sheets.
Staple the stories behind the pink circle on the left side.
Paste the last sheet to the bear's tummy.

5. Collect bears from several students. Cut a paper bag cover in the same shape. Hinge it on the left arm. Punch two holes and use paper fasteners to hold it all together.

Peek under the Mushroom

Writing Suggestions

1. Under the Magic Mushroom
   I found a fairy circle of mushrooms in the moonlight. When I peeked under the biggest one I found . . .

2. Leprechaun's Lost Treasure
   Little leprechaun hid his treasure under a mushroom, but he is so forgetful he can't remember which one. Can you help him?

3. What can you do with a mushroom?
   Try to think of a good or unusual use for this mushroom.

Steps

1.
   Begin with yellow construction paper for the background.

2.
   Cut a mushroom shape from white construction paper.
   Fold back the top of the mushroom.

3.
   Paste this flap to the right side of the yellow paper.

   Save the left side of the paper for the story about the mushroom. Paste it on whenever it's completed.

4. Add details to the picture that add interest and enrich the story.
   Lift the mushroom flap and draw a surprise under it.

5.
   Collect pages from several students.
   Add a cover and staple it together on the left.
   Cover the spine with cloth tape.

Sunny Side Up

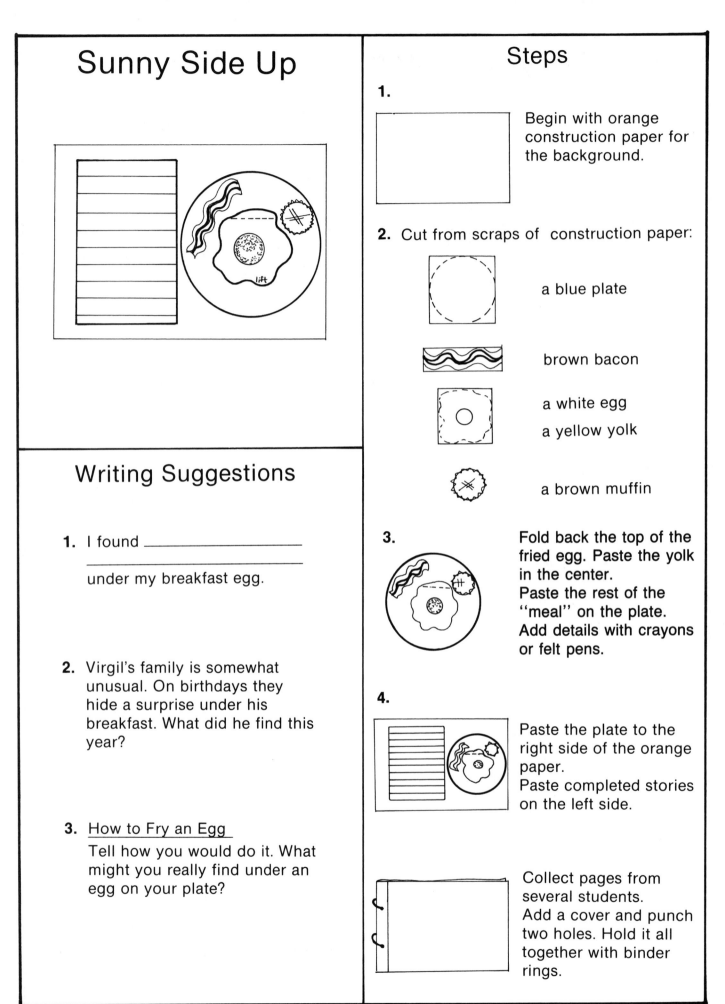

Writing Suggestions

1. I found _____

   _____

   under my breakfast egg.

2. Virgil's family is somewhat unusual. On birthdays they hide a surprise under his breakfast. What did he find this year?

3. How to Fry an Egg

   Tell how you would do it. What might you really find under an egg on your plate?

Steps

1.

   Begin with orange construction paper for the background.

2. Cut from scraps of construction paper:

   a blue plate

   brown bacon

   a white egg
   a yellow yolk

   a brown muffin

3.

   Fold back the top of the fried egg. Paste the yolk in the center.
   Paste the rest of the "meal" on the plate.
   Add details with crayons or felt pens.

4.

   Paste the plate to the right side of the orange paper.
   Paste completed stories on the left side.

   Collect pages from several students.
   Add a cover and punch two holes. Hold it all together with binder rings.

Swiss Cheese Surprise

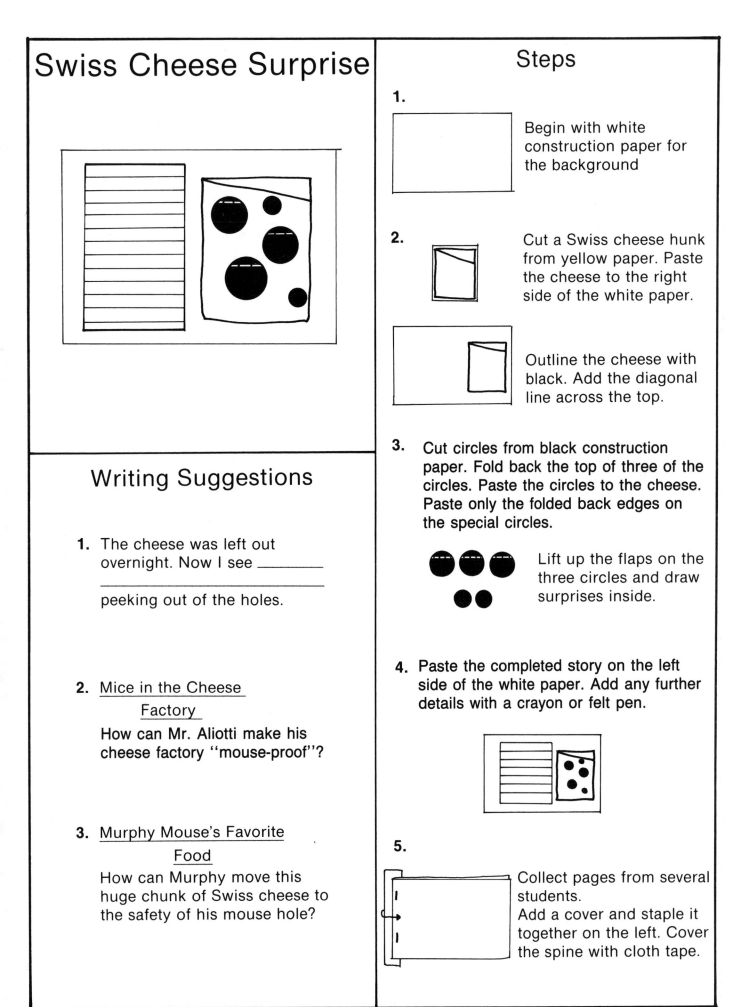

Writing Suggestions

1. The cheese was left out overnight. Now I see _____
_____
peeking out of the holes.

2. <u>Mice in the Cheese</u>
      <u>Factory</u>
How can Mr. Aliotti make his cheese factory ''mouse-proof''?

3. <u>Murphy Mouse's Favorite</u>
      <u>Food</u>
How can Murphy move this huge chunk of Swiss cheese to the safety of his mouse hole?

Steps

1. Begin with white construction paper for the background

2. Cut a Swiss cheese hunk from yellow paper. Paste the cheese to the right side of the white paper.

Outline the cheese with black. Add the diagonal line across the top.

3. Cut circles from black construction paper. Fold back the top of three of the circles. Paste the circles to the cheese. Paste only the folded back edges on the special circles.

Lift up the flaps on the three circles and draw surprises inside.

4. Paste the completed story on the left side of the white paper. Add any further details with a crayon or felt pen.

5. Collect pages from several students.
Add a cover and staple it together on the left. Cover the spine with cloth tape.

The Ghost in Sneakers

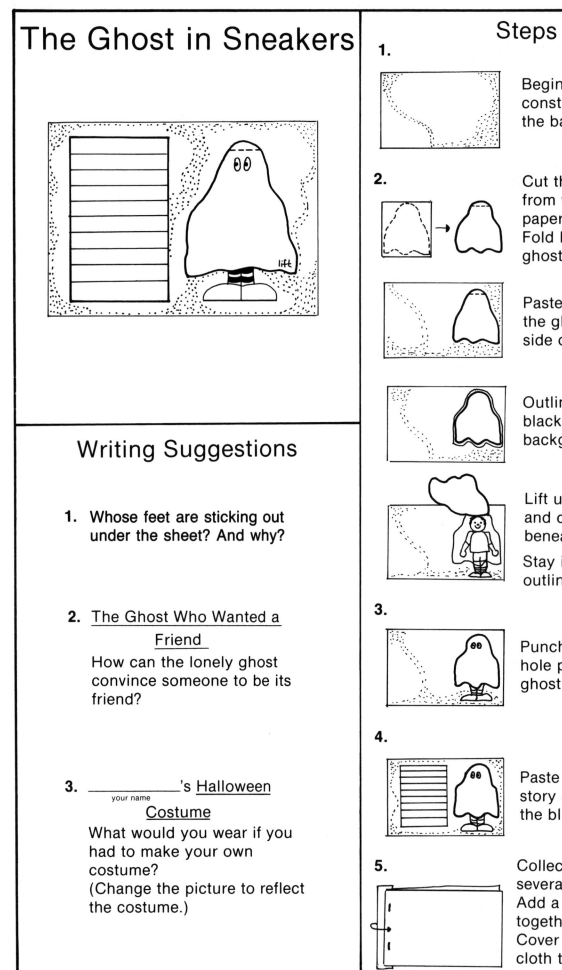

Writing Suggestions

1. **Whose feet are sticking out under the sheet? And why?**

2. <u>The Ghost Who Wanted a Friend</u>
   How can the lonely ghost convince someone to be its friend?

3. _____'s <u>Halloween</u>
   _{your name}
   <u>Costume</u>
   What would you wear if you had to make your own costume?
   (Change the picture to reflect the costume.)

Steps

1. Begin with blue construction paper for the background.

2. Cut the ghost shape from white construction paper.
   Fold back the top of the ghost flap.

   Paste the top edge of the ghost to the right side of the blue paper.

   Outline the ghost with black crayon on the background paper.

   Lift up the ghost flap and draw the "goblin" beneath.
   Stay inside the black outline.

3. Punch two holes with a hole punch to give the ghost see-through eyes.

4. Paste the completed story on the left side of the blue paper.

5. Collect pages from several students.
   Add a cover and staple it together on the left.
   Cover the spine with cloth tape.

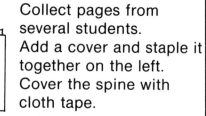

The Refrigerator

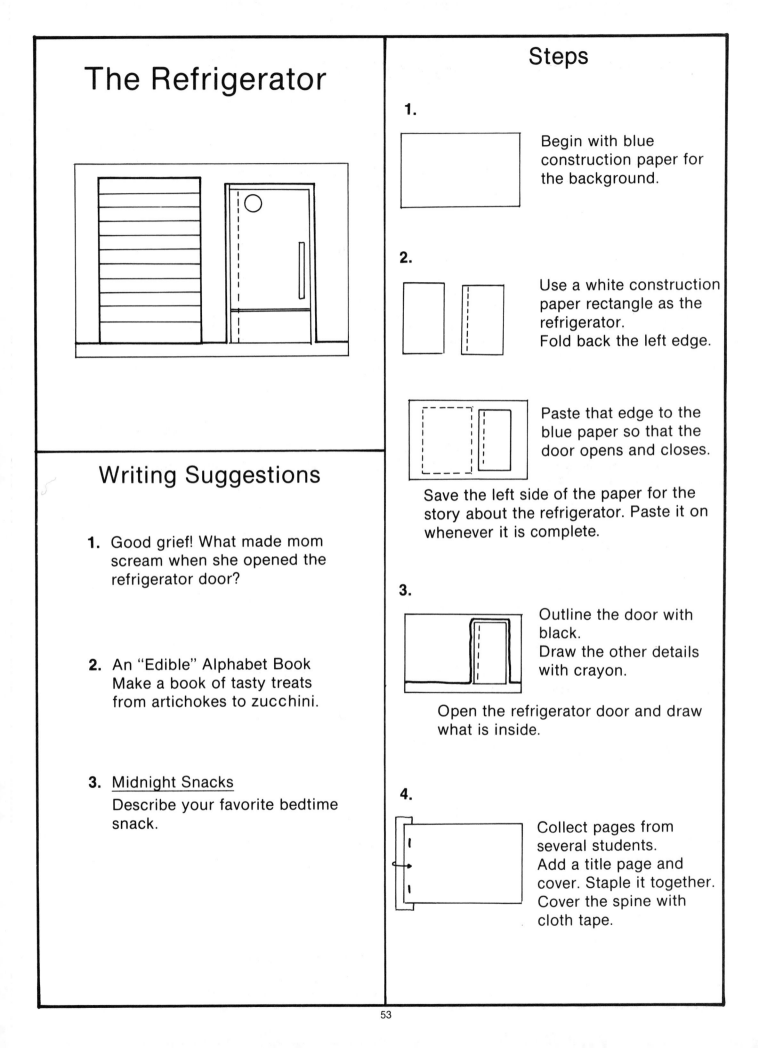

Writing Suggestions

1. Good grief! What made mom scream when she opened the refrigerator door?

2. An "Edible" Alphabet Book
Make a book of tasty treats from artichokes to zucchini.

3. <u>Midnight Snacks</u>
Describe your favorite bedtime snack.

Steps

1.

Begin with blue construction paper for the background.

2.

Use a white construction paper rectangle as the refrigerator.
Fold back the left edge.

Paste that edge to the blue paper so that the door opens and closes.

Save the left side of the paper for the story about the refrigerator. Paste it on whenever it is complete.

3.

Outline the door with black.
Draw the other details with crayon.

Open the refrigerator door and draw what is inside.

4.

Collect pages from several students.
Add a title page and cover. Staple it together.
Cover the spine with cloth tape.

PULL-TAB BOOKS

Children of all ages love "mechanical" books. Pull-tabs add a special element to stories and illustrations.

This is an area where practice by the teacher beforehand is very important as the steps need to be followed carefully.

Writing suggestions and patterns are included for each pull-tab project. The pull-tabs should be run on construction paper or tag for added durability. Teachers of primary students should cut the slits before the lesson. The slit can be reinforced by placing tape on the back.

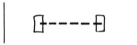

An overhead projector is perfect for showing the drawing steps. If none is available, drawing steps can be put on the chalkboard.

Pages can be used to illustrate short stories in a group book or as one form of illustration in an individual book.

Pull-tab illustrations and stories may be glued to a sheet of construction paper. Pages can then be put into a book. (See page 4.)

Pull-tabs can also be turned into charming greeting cards!

The Wagging Dog

Writing Suggestions

1. Why is Spotty's tail wagging?

2. <u>How to Name a Dog</u>
Imagine you have a new dog. What would you name it? Why would this be a good name for the dog?

3. <u>A Bark in the Night</u>
The sound of a dog barking wakes you up in the middle of the night.

4. <u>How to Care for Your Dog</u>
Pretend I don't know anything about dogs. Tell me how to take care of one.

Steps

1. Reproduce the Basic Pull-Tab Pattern on page 60. Fold it and cut the slit as marked.

2. The pattern for the pull-tab that is inserted in the slit can be found on page 61.

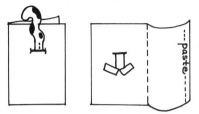

Insert the pull tab into the slit. Reach inside the folded pattern and cut on the dotted line. Fold each of the pieces to the side. That secures the tab to keep it from falling out.
Paste the folder closed along outside edge.

3. Sketch the dog's body lightly with pencil before adding color.

Add details to the picture so that it illustrates the story.

4. Paste the pull-tab pictured and accompanying story side by side on a 12" x 18" sheet of construction paper.

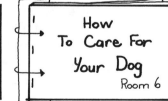

Now organize your students' stories, and design a cover. Staple them all together along the left spine. Cover with cloth tape. Did you include a title page and table of contents?

Raccoon with Tail

Writing Suggestions

1. **The Mischievous Raccoon**

   What might happen if you try to turn a wild raccoon into a tame pet?

2. **Raccoon Pests**

   Raccoons have been turning over the garbage cans and eating the dog's food. How can I stop them?

3. **All I Know About Raccoons**

   You may need to visit the library before you begin.

Steps

1. Reproduce the Basic Pull-Tab Pattern on page 60. Fold it and cut the slit as marked.

2. The pattern for the pull-tab that is inserted in the slit can be found on page 61.

   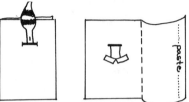

   Insert the pull-tab into the slit. Reach inside the folded pattern and cut on the dotted line. Fold each of the pieces to the side. That secures the tab to keep it from falling out.
   Paste the folder closed along the outside edge.

3. Sketch raccoon's body lightly with pencil before adding color.

   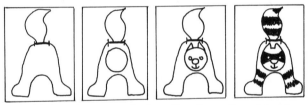

   Add background details that fit with the story that is being written.

4. Paste the pull-tab picture and accompanying story side by side on a 12'' x 18'' sheet of construction paper.

   Now organize your students' stories and design a cover. Staple them all together along the left spine. Cover with cloth tape. Did you include a title page and table of contents?

Watch the Flower Grow

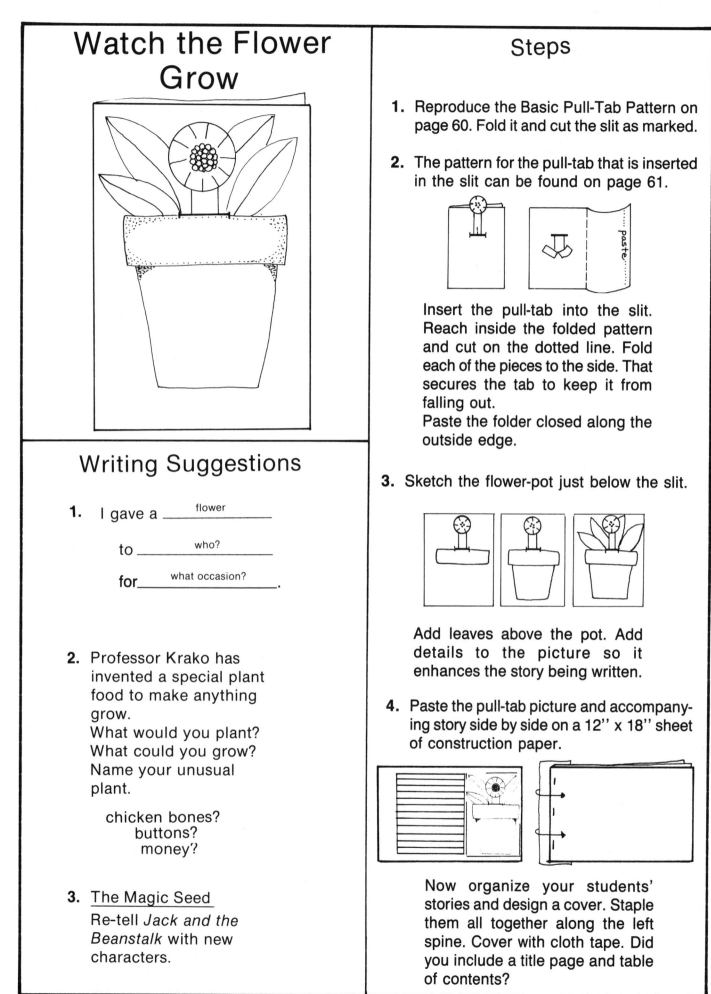

Steps

1. Reproduce the Basic Pull-Tab Pattern on page 60. Fold it and cut the slit as marked.

2. The pattern for the pull-tab that is inserted in the slit can be found on page 61.

Insert the pull-tab into the slit. Reach inside the folded pattern and cut on the dotted line. Fold each of the pieces to the side. That secures the tab to keep it from falling out.
Paste the folder closed along the outside edge.

3. Sketch the flower-pot just below the slit.

Add leaves above the pot. Add details to the picture so it enhances the story being written.

4. Paste the pull-tab picture and accompanying story side by side on a 12'' x 18'' sheet of construction paper.

Now organize your students' stories and design a cover. Staple them all together along the left spine. Cover with cloth tape. Did you include a title page and table of contents?

Writing Suggestions

1. I gave a ___flower___

to ___who?___

for___what occasion?___.

2. Professor Krako has invented a special plant food to make anything grow.
What would you plant? What could you grow? Name your unusual plant.

    chicken bones?
      buttons?
        money?

3. The Magic Seed
Re-tell *Jack and the Beanstalk* with new characters.

A Charming Snake

Writing Suggestions

1. Our Snake Book

Name and describe your favorite kind of snake.

2. The Mysterious Package

The delivery man left a mysterious package on my doorstep. Should I open it? What can it be?

3. Ahmed, the Snake Charmer

How did little Ahmed learn how to make snakes do his bidding?

Steps

1. Reproduce the Basic Pull-Tab Pattern on page 60. Fold it and cut the slit as marked.

2. The pattern for the pull-tab that is inserted in the slit can be found on page 61.

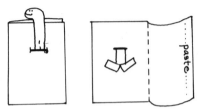

Insert the pull-tab into the slit. Reach inside the folded pattern and cut on the dotted line. Fold each of the pieces to the side. That secures the tab to keep it from falling out.
Paste the folder closed along the outside edge.

3. Sketch the basket in pencil before adding color. Add details to your picture that enhance the story being written.

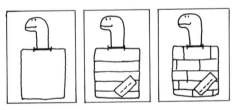

4. Paste the pull-tab picture and accompanying story side by side on a 12" x 18" sheet of construction paper.

 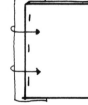

Now organize your students' stories and design a cover. Staple them all together along the left spine. Cover with cloth tape. Did you include a title page and table of contents?

Off ZOOMS the Rocket

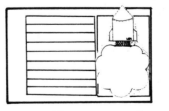

Writing Suggestions

1. <u>Countdown to Space</u>

   Create an exciting adventure for the first family in space.

2. I would (love)/(hate) to be an astronaut traveling through space.

   Give your reasons why you would enjoy or hate such a journey.

3. A rocket ship has broken down and gone off course.
   It is heading toward the Earth and cannot stop. How would you rescue the astronauts and keep the ship from crashing into a city?

Steps

1. Reproduce the Basic Pull-Tab Pattern on page 60. Fold it and cut the slit as marked.

2. The pattern for the pull-tab that is inserted in the slit can be found on page 61.

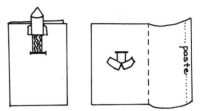

   Insert the pull-tab into the slit. Reach inside the folded pattern and cut on the dotted line. Fold each of the pieces to the side. That secures the tab to keep it from falling out.
   Paste the folder closed along the outside edge.

3. Draw the cloud just below the slit line.

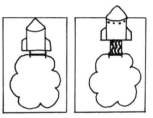

   Add details to the rocket. ZOOM lines in red and orange below the rocket on the pull-tab are effective.

4. Paste the pull-tab picture and accompanying story side by side on a 12'' x 18'' sheet of construction paper.

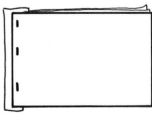

   Now organize your students' stories and design a cover. Staple them all together along the left spine. Cover with cloth tape. Did you include a title page and table of contents?

Basic Pull-Tab Book Pattern

1. Fold on
2. Cut slit. ⊢——⊣

- fold -

cut

(top)

60

Pull-Tab Insert Patterns
for pages 55, 56, 57, 58, 59

These pull tabs will last longer if reproduced on tag or construction paper.

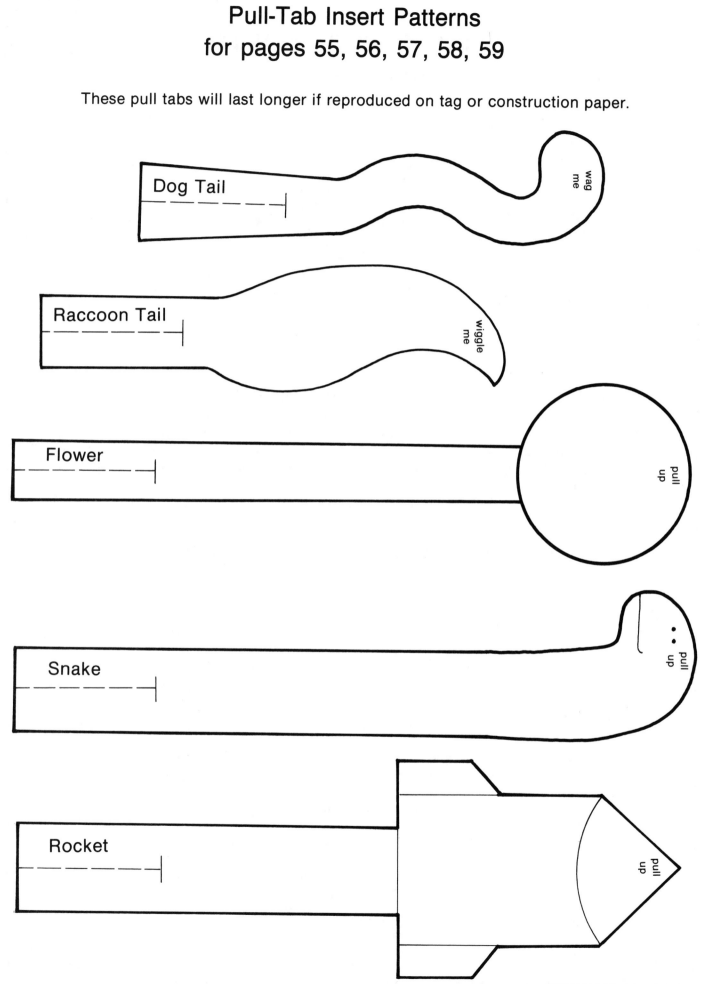

Dog Tail

wag me

Raccoon Tail

wiggle me

Flower

pull up

Snake

pull up

Rocket

pull up

BOOKS WITH WHEELS

The interest and excitement wheels add to a book make them worth a little extra effort.

A wheel can be used as one illustration in a long story, or several can be put together in a group book. Writing suggestions and pattern forms are provided for each book idea. Practice constructing a wheel and drawing the picture before trying the lesson with your class. Placement of the picture varies somewhat for each lesson. If you teach K-2 grades, you will need to put the wheels together yourself before beginning the drawing lesson.

Wheel pages should be run on construction paper. (You may even want to make the wheel portion of tag.) Place a hole reinforcer on the paper where the paper fastener goes through to add extra strength.

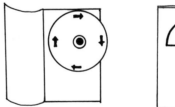
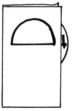

Wheel illustrations and stories may be glued to a sheet of construction paper and then put in a book. (See pages 3-4.)

The Juggler

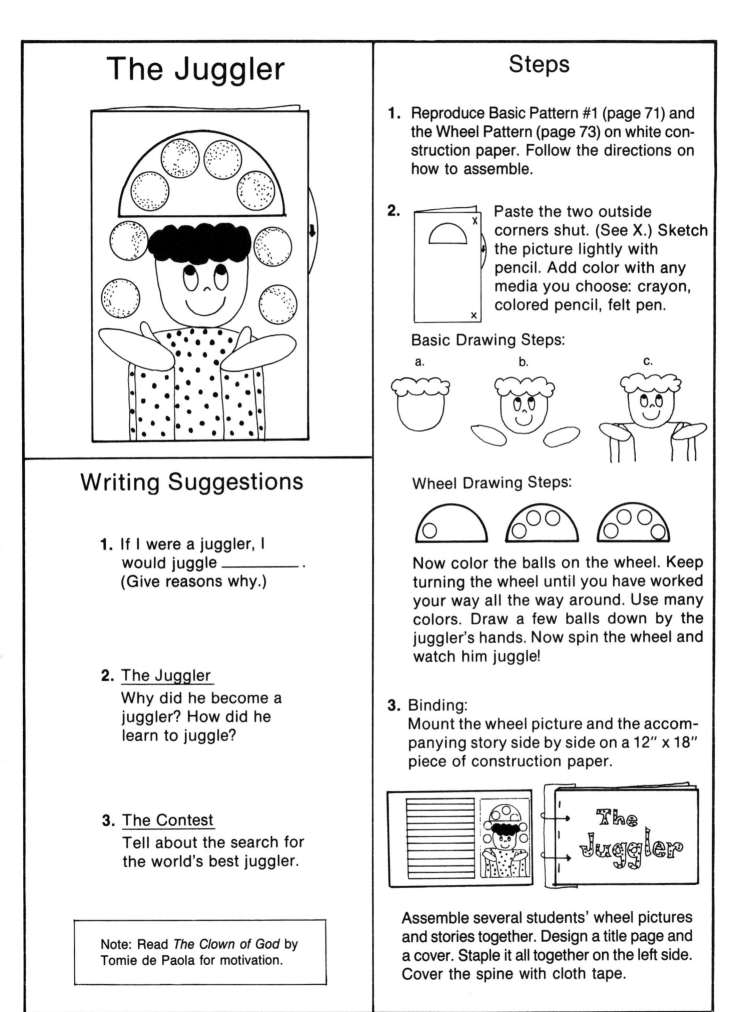

Writing Suggestions

1. If I were a juggler, I would juggle _____ .
   (Give reasons why.)

2. <u>The Juggler</u>
   Why did he become a juggler? How did he learn to juggle?

3. <u>The Contest</u>
   Tell about the search for the world's best juggler.

Note: Read *The Clown of God* by Tomie de Paola for motivation.

Steps

1. Reproduce Basic Pattern #1 (page 71) and the Wheel Pattern (page 73) on white construction paper. Follow the directions on how to assemble.

2. Paste the two outside corners shut. (See X.) Sketch the picture lightly with pencil. Add color with any media you choose: crayon, colored pencil, felt pen.

   Basic Drawing Steps:

   a.   b.   c.

   Wheel Drawing Steps:

   Now color the balls on the wheel. Keep turning the wheel until you have worked your way all the way around. Use many colors. Draw a few balls down by the juggler's hands. Now spin the wheel and watch him juggle!

3. Binding:
   Mount the wheel picture and the accompanying story side by side on a 12" x 18" piece of construction paper.

   Assemble several students' wheel pictures and stories together. Design a title page and a cover. Staple it all together on the left side. Cover the spine with cloth tape.

Four & Twenty Blackbirds

Writing Suggestions

1. Four and twenty blackbirds were baked in a pie. When the pie was opened, the birds began to _____ .

2. The King's Banquet
   What else did the King have at his banquet besides bird pie?

3. Peculiar Pies
   Create your own unusual pie. What are the ingredients? To whom would you serve it?

Steps

1. Reproduce Basic Pattern #1 (page 71) and the Wheel Pattern (page 73) on white construction paper. Follow the directions on how to assemble.

2. Paste the two outside corners shut. (See X.) Sketch the picture lightly with pencil. Add color with any media you choose: crayon, colored pencil, felt pen.

   Basic Drawing Steps:

   a.   b.

   Wheel Drawing Steps:

   a.
   b.
   c.
   Draw the birds on the wheel. Keep turning the wheel until you have worked your way all the way around. Color the birds black with orange heads.

3. Binding:
   Mount the wheel picture and the accompanying story side by side on a 12" x 18" piece of construction paper.

   Assemble several students' wheel pictures and stories together. Design a title page and a cover. Staple it all together on the left side. Cover the spine with cloth tape.

The Active Octopus

Writing Suggestions

1. <u>The Shy Octopus</u>

Where and how could an octopus hide from strangers?

2. <u>Inky to the Rescue</u>

This brave octopus races to the rescue of the injured diver.

3. If you had eight arms, what would you do?

Steps

1. Reproduce Basic Pattern #1 (page 71) and the Wheel Pattern (page 73) on white construction paper. Follow the directions on how to assemble.

2. Paste the two outside corners shut. (See X.) Sketch the picture lightly with pencil. Add color with any media you choose: crayon, colored pencil, felt pen.

Basic Drawing Steps:

a.
b.
c.

Wheel Drawing Steps:

Draw the tentacles on the wheel. Keep turning the wheel until you have drawn tentacles all the way around. Draw the suction cups on the tentacles.

3. Binding:

Mount the wheel picture and the accompanying story side by side on a 12" x 18" piece of construction paper.

Assemble several students' wheel pictures and stories together. Design a title page and a cover. Staple it all together on the left side. Cover the spine with cloth tape.

The Dancer

Writing Suggestions

1. **Dancing Feet**

   Tell about your favorite kind of dancing. (Make your picture match your story.)

2. **Twinkle-Toes**

   Betsy is nicknamed "twinkle-toes." Can you tell why?

3. **On Stage**

   It's Tonya's big chance to perform on stage, but she has a big problem.

Steps

1. Reproduce Basic Pattern #1 (page 71) and the Wheel Pattern (page 73) on white construction paper. Follow the directions on how to assemble.

2. 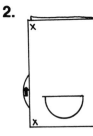 Paste the two outside corners shut. (See X.) Sketch the picture lightly with pencil. Add color with any media you choose: crayon, colored pencil, felt pen.

Basic Drawing Steps:

a.   b.   c.

 Draw the dancer's legs on the wheel.
Keep drawing them until you have gone all the way around. Spin the wheel and watch her dance!

3. Binding:
   Mount the wheel picture and the accompanying story side by side on a 12″ x 18″ piece of construction paper.

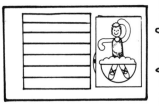 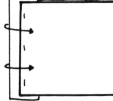

Assemble several students' wheel pictures and stories together. Design a title page and a cover. Staple it all together on the left side. Cover the spine with cloth tape.

Weather Changes from Sunny to Stormy

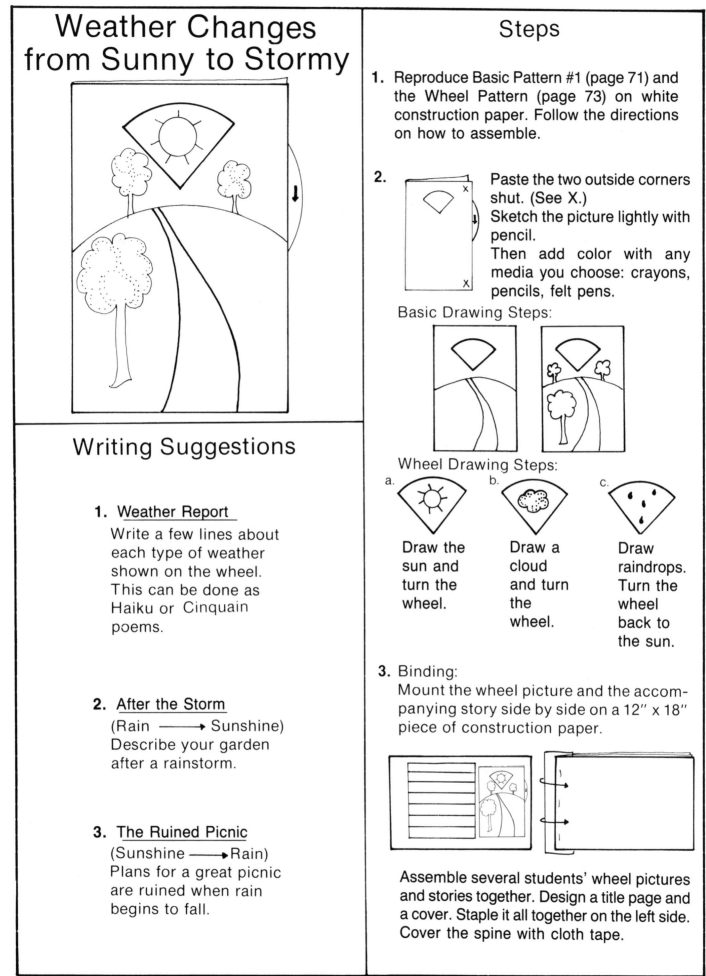

Writing Suggestions

1. Weather Report

Write a few lines about each type of weather shown on the wheel. This can be done as Haiku or Cinquain poems.

2. After the Storm

(Rain ⟶ Sunshine) Describe your garden after a rainstorm.

3. The Ruined Picnic

(Sunshine ⟶ Rain) Plans for a great picnic are ruined when rain begins to fall.

Steps

1. Reproduce Basic Pattern #1 (page 71) and the Wheel Pattern (page 73) on white construction paper. Follow the directions on how to assemble.

2. Paste the two outside corners shut. (See X.) Sketch the picture lightly with pencil. Then add color with any media you choose: crayons, pencils, felt pens.

Basic Drawing Steps:

Wheel Drawing Steps:

a. Draw the sun and turn the wheel.

b. Draw a cloud and turn the wheel.

c. Draw raindrops. Turn the wheel back to the sun.

3. Binding:
Mount the wheel picture and the accompanying story side by side on a 12″ x 18″ piece of construction paper.

Assemble several students' wheel pictures and stories together. Design a title page and a cover. Staple it all together on the left side. Cover the spine with cloth tape.

A Spouting Whale

Writing Suggestions

1. A whale can _____.
                (action)

2. <u>Whale in My Bathtub</u>
What would happen if your rubber whale suddenly came alive?

3. <u>Migration</u>
Either write reports on whale migration or fiction stories about adventures along the migration route.

Steps

1. Reproduce Basic Pattern #1 (page 71) and the Wheel Pattern (page 73) on white construction paper. Follow the directions on how to assemble.

2. Paste the two outside corners shut. (See X.)
Sketch the picture lightly with pencil.
Then add color with any media you choose: crayons, , pencils, felt pens.

Basic Drawing Steps:
a.   b.   c.

Wheel Drawing Steps:
a.   b.   c.

Draw the whale spout three times so that each time it gets bigger. Spin the wheel and watch the whale spout.

3. Binding:
Mount the wheel picture and the accompanying story side by side on a 12″ x 18″ piece of construction paper.

Assemble several students' wheel pictures and stories together. Design a title page and a cover. Staple it all together on the left side. Cover the spine with cloth tape.

A Runner

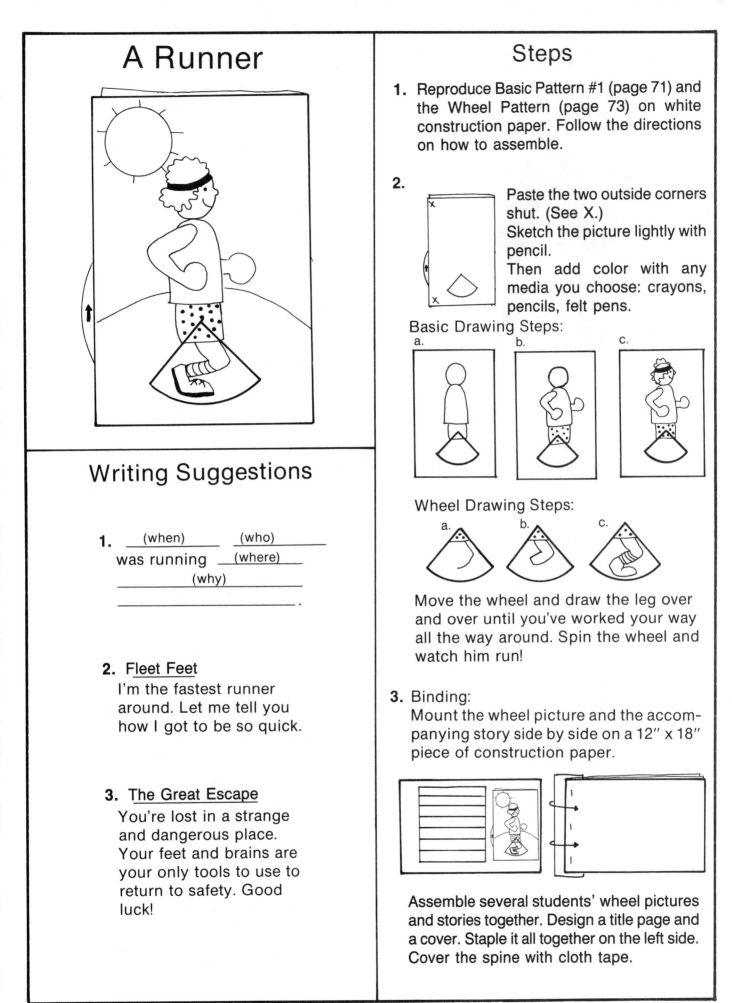

Writing Suggestions

1. _____(when)_____ ____(who)____
   was running ____(where)____
   ____(why)____
   _____.

2. **Fleet Feet**
   I'm the fastest runner around. Let me tell you how I got to be so quick.

3. **The Great Escape**
   You're lost in a strange and dangerous place. Your feet and brains are your only tools to use to return to safety. Good luck!

Steps

1. Reproduce Basic Pattern #1 (page 71) and the Wheel Pattern (page 73) on white construction paper. Follow the directions on how to assemble.

2. Paste the two outside corners shut. (See X.)
   Sketch the picture lightly with pencil.
   Then add color with any media you choose: crayons, pencils, felt pens.

   Basic Drawing Steps:
   a.   b.   c.

   Wheel Drawing Steps:
   a.   b.   c.

   Move the wheel and draw the leg over and over until you've worked your way all the way around. Spin the wheel and watch him run!

3. Binding:
   Mount the wheel picture and the accompanying story side by side on a 12″ x 18″ piece of construction paper.

   Assemble several students' wheel pictures and stories together. Design a title page and a cover. Staple it all together on the left side. Cover the spine with cloth tape.

The Penguin

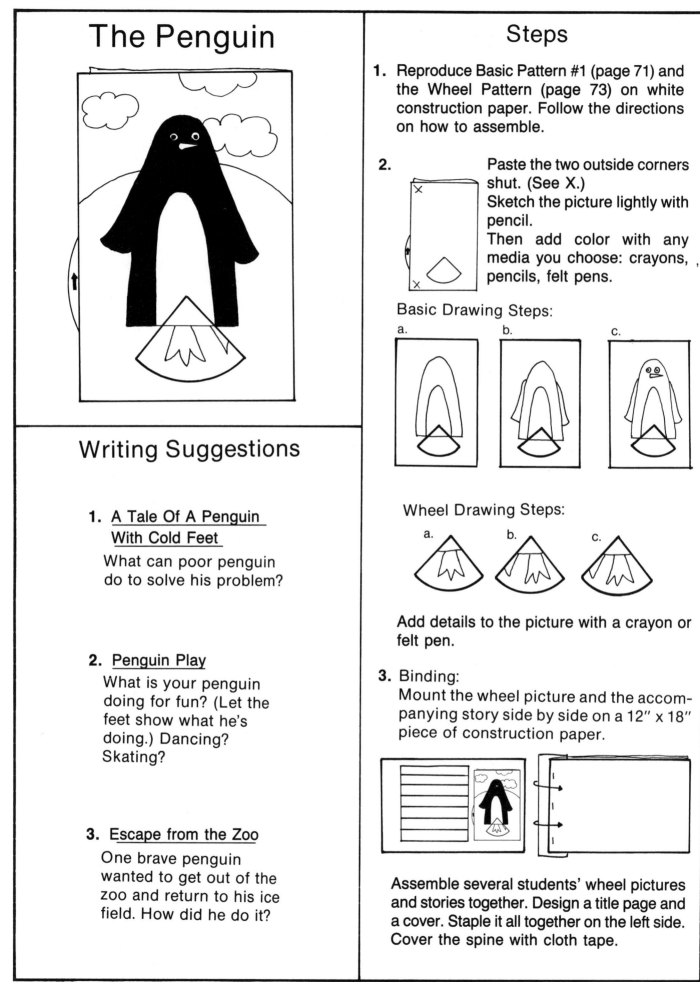

Writing Suggestions

1. <u>A Tale Of A Penguin
   With Cold Feet</u>

   What can poor penguin
   do to solve his problem?

2. <u>Penguin Play</u>

   What is your penguin
   doing for fun? (Let the
   feet show what he's
   doing.) Dancing?
   Skating?

3. <u>Escape from the Zoo</u>

   One brave penguin
   wanted to get out of the
   zoo and return to his ice
   field. How did he do it?

Steps

1. Reproduce Basic Pattern #1 (page 71) and
   the Wheel Pattern (page 73) on white
   construction paper. Follow the directions
   on how to assemble.

2. Paste the two outside corners
   shut. (See X.)
   Sketch the picture lightly with
   pencil.
   Then add color with any
   media you choose: crayons, ,
   pencils, felt pens.

Basic Drawing Steps:

a.   b.   c.

Wheel Drawing Steps:

a.   b.   c.

Add details to the picture with a crayon or
felt pen.

3. Binding:
   Mount the wheel picture and the accompanying story side by side on a 12″ x 18″
   piece of construction paper.

Assemble several students' wheel pictures
and stories together. Design a title page and
a cover. Staple it all together on the left side.
Cover the spine with cloth tape.

Basic Pattern #1 for Wheel Books

pages 63, 64, 65, 66

1. Fold on the dotted line.
2. Cut out the window with scissors or an art knife.
3. Cut out the wheel pattern (page 73) and place it behind the window.
4. Put a paper fastener through the ● on the wheel. Go through the wheel and the back cover. Secure the paper fastener.

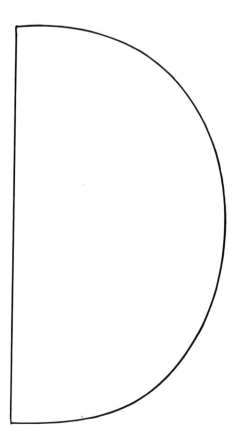

Basic Pattern #2 for Wheel Books

pages 67, 68, 69, 70

1. Fold on the dotted line.
2. Cut out the window with scissors or an art knife.
3. Cut out the wheel pattern (page 73) and place it behind the window.
4. Put a paper fastener through the • on the wheel. Go through the wheel and the back cover. Secure the paper fastener.

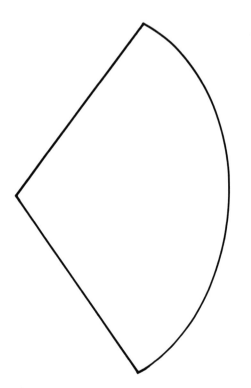

Wheel Pattern for Wheel Books

pages 63 to 70

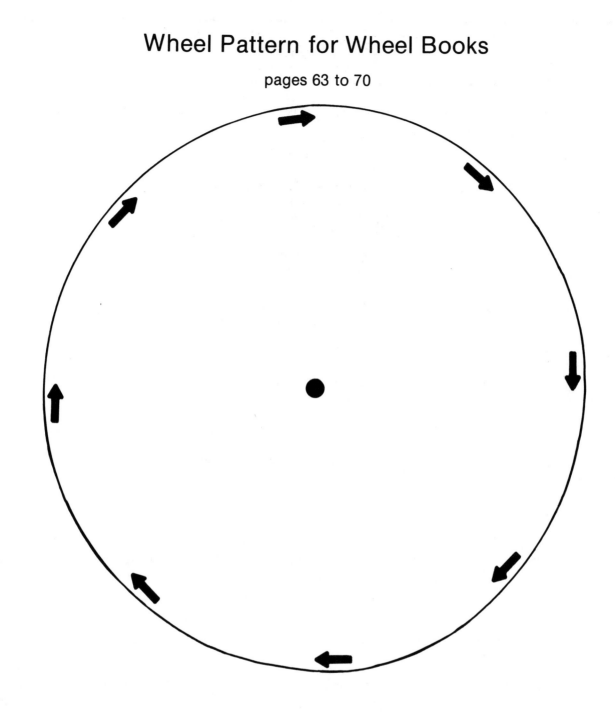

POP-UP BOOKS

Open the page and...surprise! Up pops the perfect illustration for your story, or answer to your riddle.

Writing suggestions and pattern forms are provided for each book idea. The forms should be run on construction paper, since these pages will get a lot of use.

Practice the folds before using with children. Follow the directions carefully. This is a great place to encourage children to help one another.

Pop-up pages are ideal for small group or individual stories. Too many pages are difficult to bind.

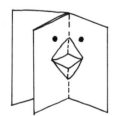

Completed pages may be pasted back-to-back and then put into a cover. (See pages 3-4.) Paste only the edges. If you get paste on the pop-up portion, it won't work.

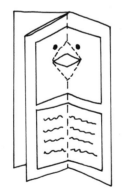

Or the completed pages may be pasted to construction paper with the story before binding. Be sure to place the page on a fold or no "popping-up" will occur. The pages are then pasted back to back as above.

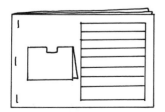

The pages may be pasted to a flat sheet of construction paper if only one side is pasted down. The pages can then be placed in a cover.

NOTE: Pop-ups make great greeting cards.

Girl with Pop-Up Hat

Writing Suggestions

1. **What is on your hat? Why did you choose these things?**

   Teacher — You may want to read *Jenny's Hat* by Keats to your class before this lesson.

2. **Maggie's Magic Hat**

   Strange things happen every time Maggie puts on her new hat. Describe what happens and why. Where did the hat come from?

3. **All Kinds of Hats**

   Instead of flowers, give your picture another type of hat (cowboy hat, helmet, fire hat, etc.) and tell about its use.

Steps

1. Duplicate Pop-Up Basic Pattern #1 on page 85. Follow the folding instructions.

2. Open the folded pattern.

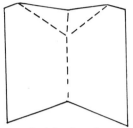

   Use a folded sheet of 12'' x 18'' construction paper as a cover. Glue the Pop-Up sheet at the top. Do NOT paste down the pop-up portion. Paste the student's story below.

   Drawing Steps:

   a.   b.   c.

   Now create all the wonderful and wild surprises on her hat.

3.

   Use a folded sheet of 12" x 18" construction paper as a cover. Glue the Pop Up sheet at the top. DO NOT paste down the pop up portion. Paste the student's story below.

NOTE: See page 4 for directions on how to put these pages together into a class book.

Pop-Up Bird with Worm

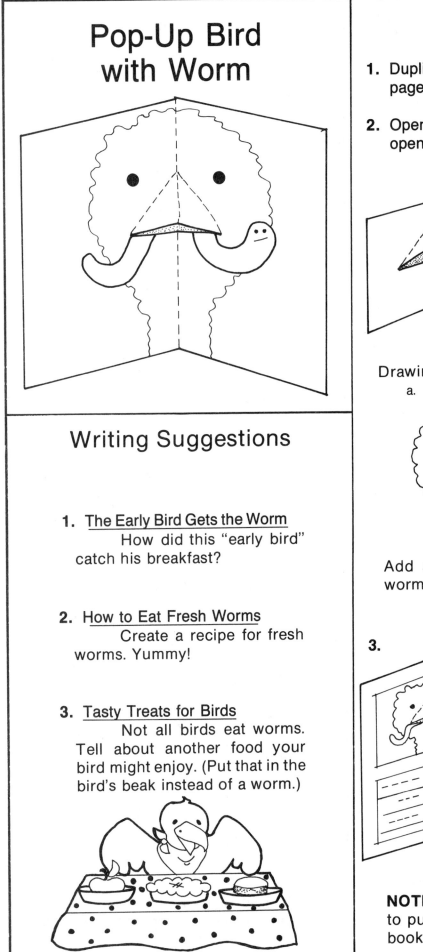

Writing Suggestions

1. <u>The Early Bird Gets the Worm</u>
How did this "early bird" catch his breakfast?

2. <u>How to Eat Fresh Worms</u>
Create a recipe for fresh worms. Yummy!

3. <u>Tasty Treats for Birds</u>
Not all birds eat worms. Tell about another food your bird might enjoy. (Put that in the bird's beak instead of a worm.)

Steps

1. Duplicate Pop-Up Basic Pattern #2 on page 86. Follow the folding instructions.

2. Open the folded pattern so the beak-like opening is on the top.

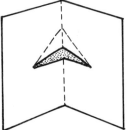

Sketch the bird and worm with pencil before adding color. Use crayons, colored pencils, collage or whatever media you choose.

Drawing Steps:

a. 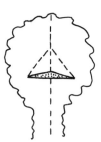   b.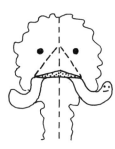

Add any details that make the bird & worm better illustrate the matching story.

3.

Use a folded sheet of 12'' x 18'' red or orange construction paper as a cover. Glue the pop-up sheet on top. Do NOT paste the portion that pops up. Paste the story below the picture.

NOTE: See page 4 for directions on how to put these pages together into a class book.

Pop-Up Gulping Fish

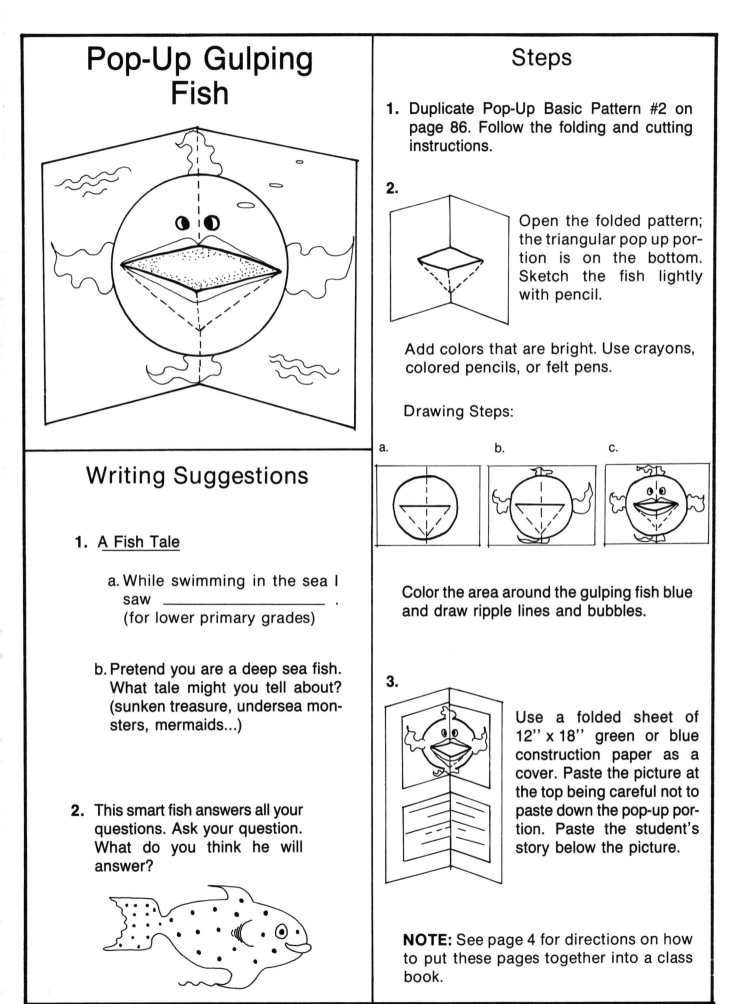

Writing Suggestions

1. A Fish Tale

    a. While swimming in the sea I
       saw _____ .
       (for lower primary grades)

    b. Pretend you are a deep sea fish.
       What tale might you tell about?
       (sunken treasure, undersea mon-
       sters, mermaids...)

2. This smart fish answers all your
    questions. Ask your question.
    What do you think he will
    answer?

Steps

1. Duplicate Pop-Up Basic Pattern #2 on page 86. Follow the folding and cutting instructions.

2.

Open the folded pattern; the triangular pop up portion is on the bottom. Sketch the fish lightly with pencil.

Add colors that are bright. Use crayons, colored pencils, or felt pens.

Drawing Steps:

a.   b.   c.

Color the area around the gulping fish blue and draw ripple lines and bubbles.

3.

Use a folded sheet of 12'' x 18'' green or blue construction paper as a cover. Paste the picture at the top being careful not to paste down the pop-up portion. Paste the student's story below the picture.

NOTE: See page 4 for directions on how to put these pages together into a class book.

Pop-Up Monkey

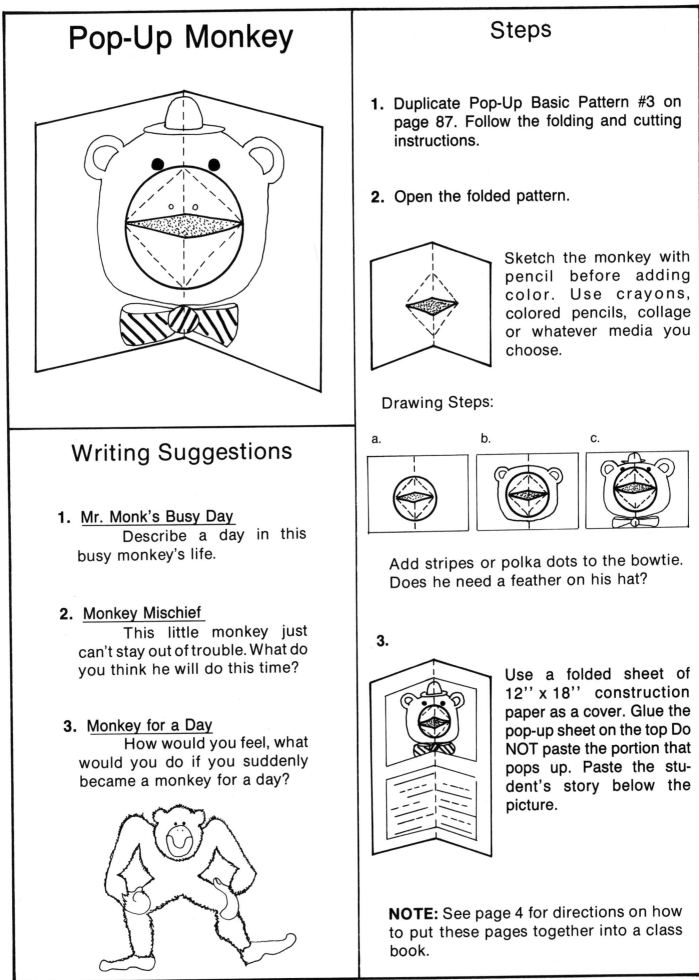

Steps

1. Duplicate Pop-Up Basic Pattern #3 on page 87. Follow the folding and cutting instructions.

2. Open the folded pattern.

Sketch the monkey with pencil before adding color. Use crayons, colored pencils, collage or whatever media you choose.

Drawing Steps:

a. b. c.

Add stripes or polka dots to the bowtie. Does he need a feather on his hat?

3.

Use a folded sheet of 12'' x 18'' construction paper as a cover. Glue the pop-up sheet on the top Do NOT paste the portion that pops up. Paste the student's story below the picture.

NOTE: See page 4 for directions on how to put these pages together into a class book.

Writing Suggestions

1. Mr. Monk's Busy Day
   Describe a day in this busy monkey's life.

2. Monkey Mischief
   This little monkey just can't stay out of trouble. What do you think he will do this time?

3. Monkey for a Day
   How would you feel, what would you do if you suddenly became a monkey for a day?

Bird with Pop-Up Beak

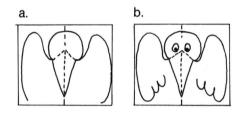

Steps

1. Duplicate Pop-Up Basic Pattern #4 on page 88. Follow the folding and cutting instructions.

2. Open the folded pattern.

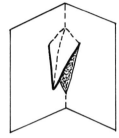

Sketch the bird with pencil before adding color. Use crayons, colored pencils, collage, or whatever media you choose.

Drawing Steps:

a.   b.

Add whatever details you need to personalize this illustration and to make it fit with your story plot.

3.

Use a folded sheet of 12'' x 18'' construction paper as a cover. Glue the pop-up sheet on top. Do NOT paste the portion that pops up. Paste the student's story below the picture.

NOTE: See page 4 for directions on how to put these pages together into a class book.

Writing Suggestions

1. <u>The Adventures of Big Beak</u>
Big Beak leads an exciting life. Imagine an adventure he might have.

2. Give your bird a name. Describe it. Tell what it can do.

3. What does it mean?
Select one figure of speech about birds. Tell what it means. (Birds of a feather flock together. A bird in the hand is worth two in the bush. The early bird catches the worm.)

Two Flying Birds with Pop-Up Beaks

Writing Suggestions

1. **Feathered Friends**
   Why are these two birds best friends?

2. **The Travels of Beaky and Bill**
   Where are these adventurous two off to now? What will happen on their journey?

3. **Riddles about Birds**
   Write your own riddle about birds. Write the answer inside one bird's beak.

Steps

1. Duplicate Pop-Up Basic Pattern #5 on page 89. Follow the folding and cutting instructions.

2. Open the folded pattern.

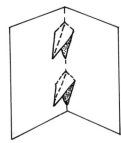

Sketch the birds with pencil before adding color. Use crayons, colored pencils, collage, or whatever media you choose.

Drawing Steps:

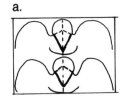 

Add some color to the sky. Are there clouds, rainbows, or any other details that make this illustration better fit the story?

3.

Use a folded sheet of 12'' x 18'' construction paper as a cover. Glue the pop-up sheet on the top Do NOT paste the portion that pops up. Paste the student's story below the picture.

NOTE: See page 4 for directions on how to put these pages together into a class book.

The Pop-Up Wolf

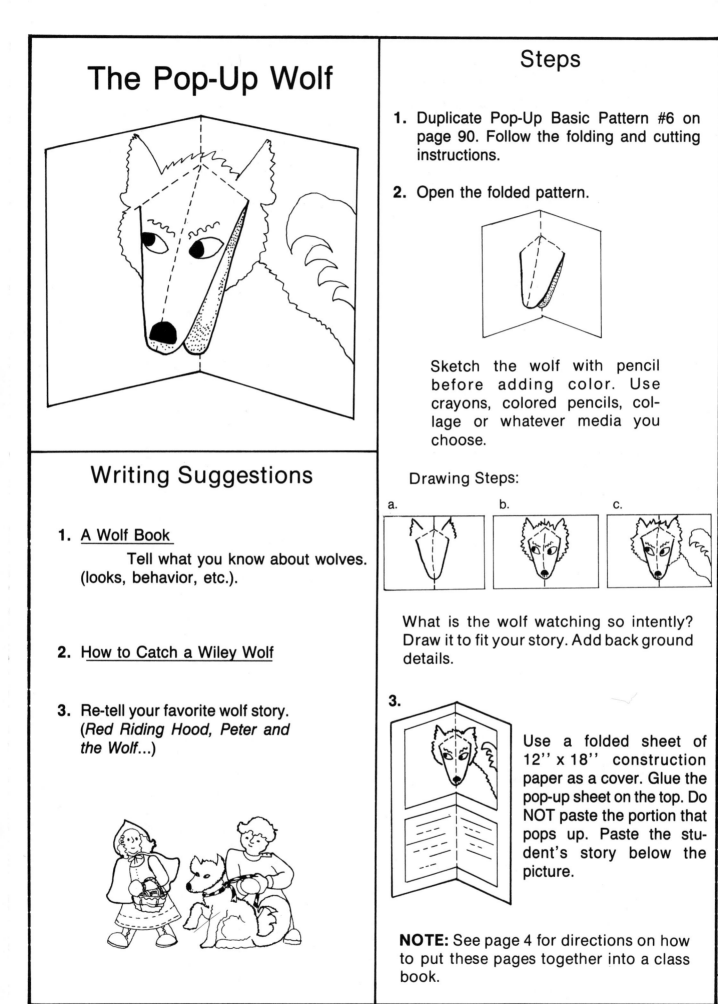

Writing Suggestions

1. <u>A Wolf Book</u>

    Tell what you know about wolves. (looks, behavior, etc.).

2. <u>How to Catch a Wiley Wolf</u>

3. Re-tell your favorite wolf story. (*Red Riding Hood, Peter and the Wolf*...)

Steps

1. Duplicate Pop-Up Basic Pattern #6 on page 90. Follow the folding and cutting instructions.

2. Open the folded pattern.

    Sketch the wolf with pencil before adding color. Use crayons, colored pencils, collage or whatever media you choose.

    Drawing Steps:

    a. b. c.

    What is the wolf watching so intently? Draw it to fit your story. Add back ground details.

3. Use a folded sheet of 12'' x 18'' construction paper as a cover. Glue the pop-up sheet on the top. Do NOT paste the portion that pops up. Paste the student's story below the picture.

NOTE: See page 4 for directions on how to put these pages together into a class book.

Pop-Up Riddle Book

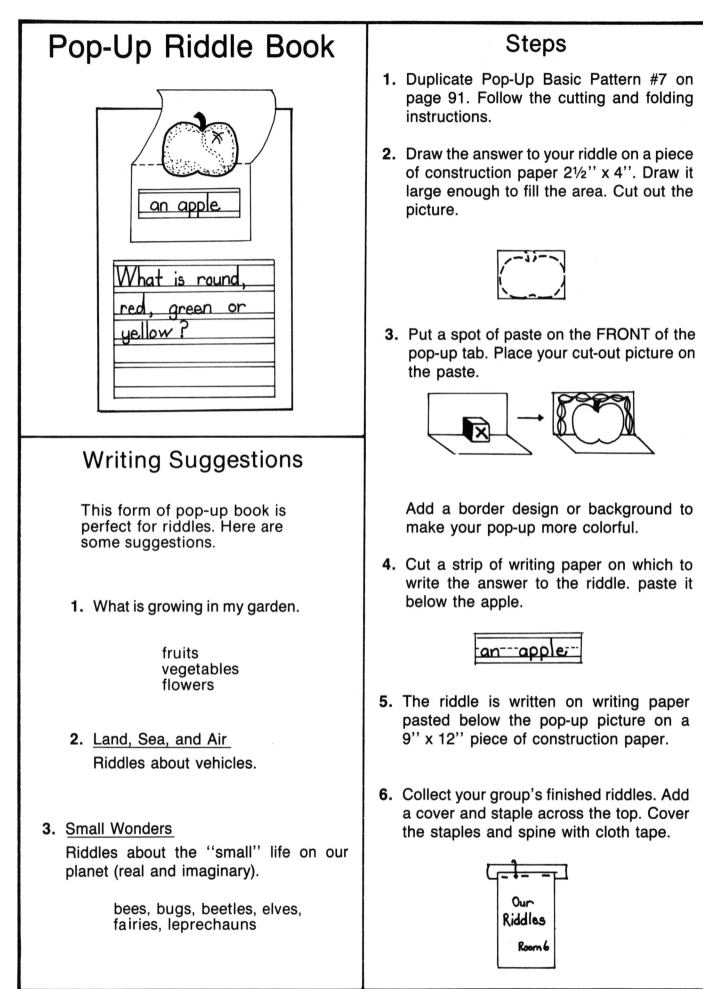

Writing Suggestions

This form of pop-up book is perfect for riddles. Here are some suggestions.

1. What is growing in my garden.

    fruits
    vegetables
    flowers

2. Land, Sea, and Air

    Riddles about vehicles.

3. Small Wonders

    Riddles about the "small" life on our planet (real and imaginary).

    bees, bugs, beetles, elves, fairies, leprechauns

Steps

1. Duplicate Pop-Up Basic Pattern #7 on page 91. Follow the cutting and folding instructions.

2. Draw the answer to your riddle on a piece of construction paper 2½'' x 4''. Draw it large enough to fill the area. Cut out the picture.

3. Put a spot of paste on the FRONT of the pop-up tab. Place your cut-out picture on the paste.

   Add a border design or background to make your pop-up more colorful.

4. Cut a strip of writing paper on which to write the answer to the riddle. paste it below the apple.

5. The riddle is written on writing paper pasted below the pop-up picture on a 9'' x 12'' piece of construction paper.

6. Collect your group's finished riddles. Add a cover and staple across the top. Cover the staples and spine with cloth tape.

Pop-Up Alphabet Book

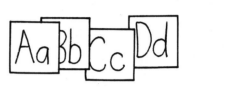

Steps

1. Duplicate Pop-Up Basic Pattern #8 on page 92. Follow the cutting and folding instructions.

2. Cut construction paper squares 3" x 3". Write a different letter of the alphabet on each one. Give one to each student. Also give the student a 3" x 4" piece of construction paper on which to illustrate a letter of the alphabet. They may cut out these forms after coloring them.

Open the pop-up pattern page. Place paste on the FRONT of the pop-up tab. Place the alphabet letter and picture on the paste.

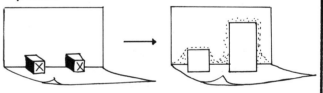

3. Students write a sentence explaining their letter on a strip of handwriting paper 2" x 7". Paste it on the bottom of the pop-up pattern page.

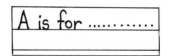

4. Collect student pages and palce in alphabetical order. Paste the back of page A to the front of page B and so on until all the pages hold together in a book.

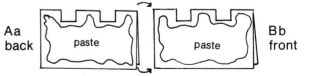

Then cut a piece of 9" x 12" construction paper to fit as a cover. Paste it in place.

Writing Suggestions

1. <u>1, 2, 3, Count With Me</u>
   Follow the same idea as the alphabet book putting a numeral on one pop-up section and a set of objects on the other. With older children you may want to write a sentence that rhymes.

6 little fish
swimming in a dish

2. <u>Opposites</u>
   Place pictures on pop-up tabs that illustrate opposites. Write sentences below.

A mouse is small.
An elephant is large.

Bunches of Animals Pop-Up Book

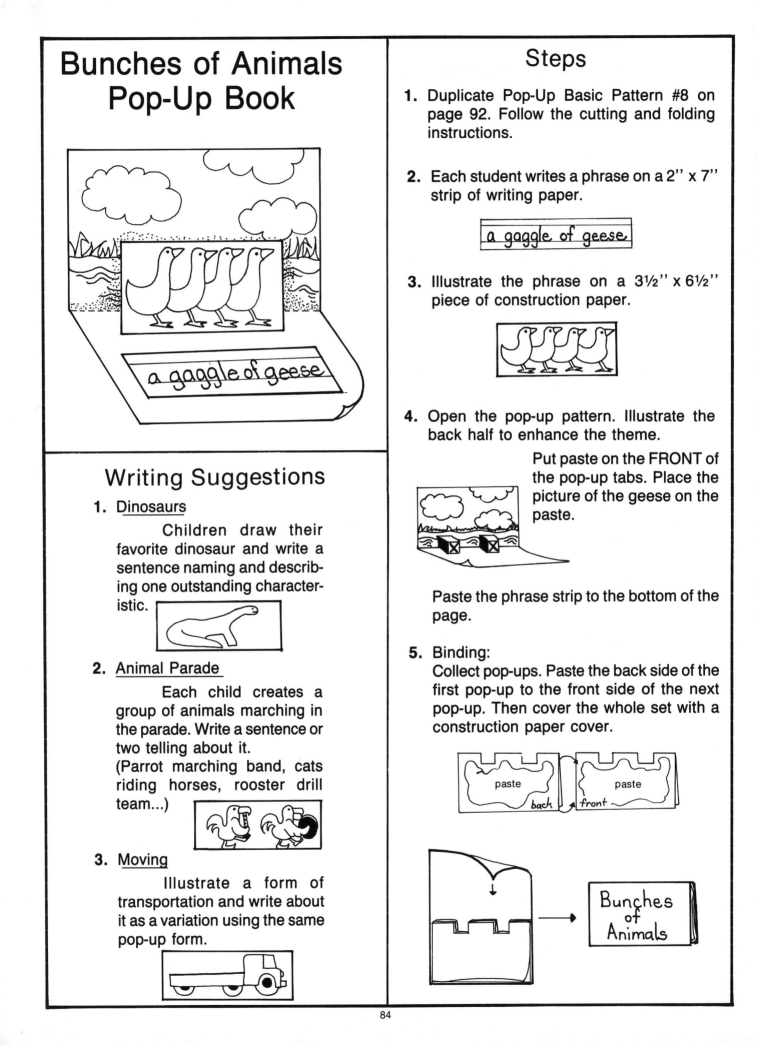

Steps

1. Duplicate Pop-Up Basic Pattern #8 on page 92. Follow the cutting and folding instructions.

2. Each student writes a phrase on a 2" x 7" strip of writing paper.

   a gaggle of geese

3. Illustrate the phrase on a 3½" x 6½" piece of construction paper.

4. Open the pop-up pattern. Illustrate the back half to enhance the theme.

   Put paste on the FRONT of the pop-up tabs. Place the picture of the geese on the paste.

   Paste the phrase strip to the bottom of the page.

5. Binding:
   Collect pop-ups. Paste the back side of the first pop-up to the front side of the next pop-up. Then cover the whole set with a construction paper cover.

Writing Suggestions

1. Dinosaurs

   Children draw their favorite dinosaur and write a sentence naming and describing one outstanding characteristic.

2. Animal Parade

   Each child creates a group of animals marching in the parade. Write a sentence or two telling about it.
   (Parrot marching band, cats riding horses, rooster drill team...)

3. Moving

   Illustrate a form of transportation and write about it as a variation using the same pop-up form.

Pop-Up Basic Pattern #1

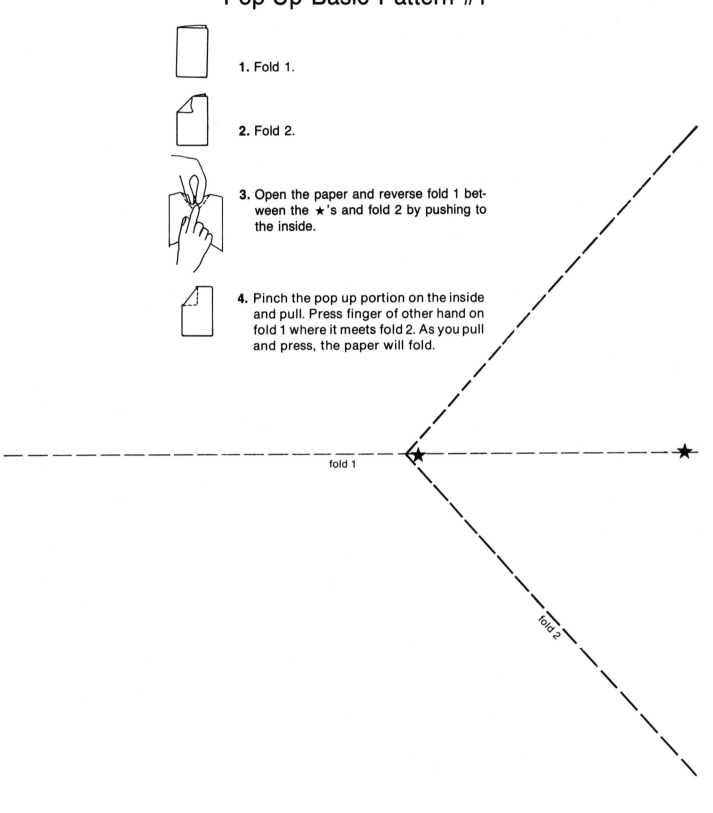

1. Fold 1.

2. Fold 2.

3. Open the paper and reverse fold 1 between the ★'s and fold 2 by pushing to the inside.

4. Pinch the pop up portion on the inside and pull. Press finger of other hand on fold 1 where it meets fold 2. As you pull and press, the paper will fold.

fold 1

fold 2

Pop-Up Basic Pattern #2

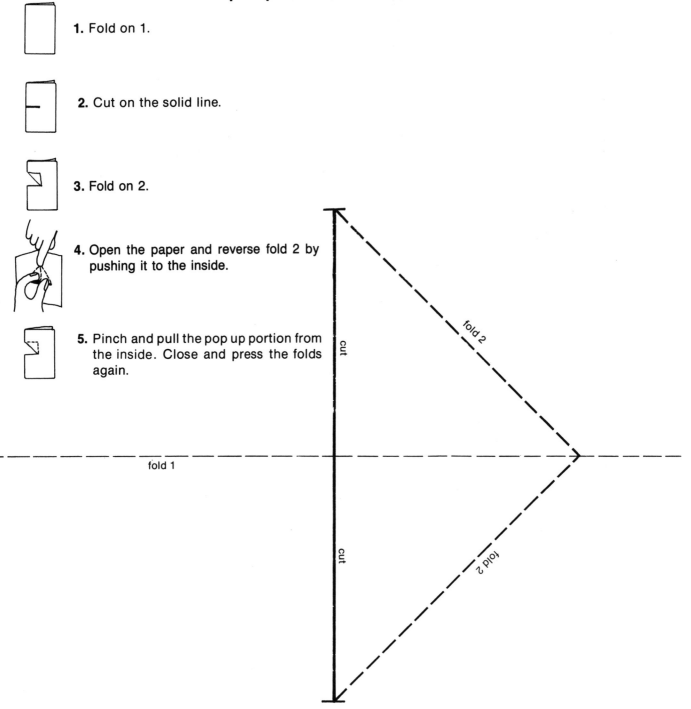

1. Fold on 1.

2. Cut on the solid line.

3. Fold on 2.

4. Open the paper and reverse fold 2 by pushing it to the inside.

5. Pinch and pull the pop up portion from the inside. Close and press the folds again.

cut

fold 2

fold 1

cut

fold 2

Pop-Up Basic Pattern #3

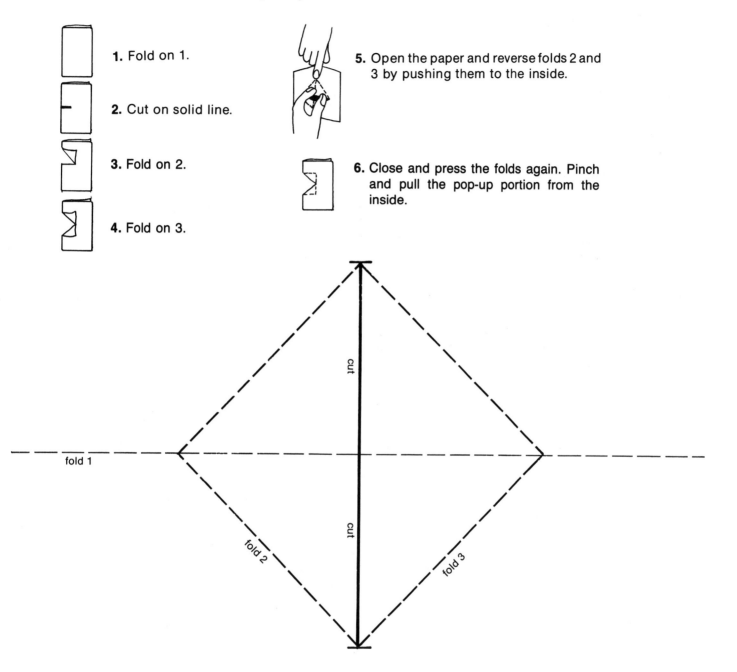

1. Fold on 1.

2. Cut on solid line.

3. Fold on 2.

4. Fold on 3.

5. Open the paper and reverse folds 2 and 3 by pushing them to the inside.

6. Close and press the folds again. Pinch and pull the pop-up portion from the inside.

fold 1

cut

cut

fold 2

fold 3

Pop-Up Basic Pattern #4

1. Fold on 1.

2. Cut on solid line.

3. Fold on 2.

4. Open paper and push pop-up to the inside. <u>Reverse</u> fold 1 (on pop-up portion) and fold 2. Hold fold 1 at the top. Pinch the pop-up.

5. Close and press folds.

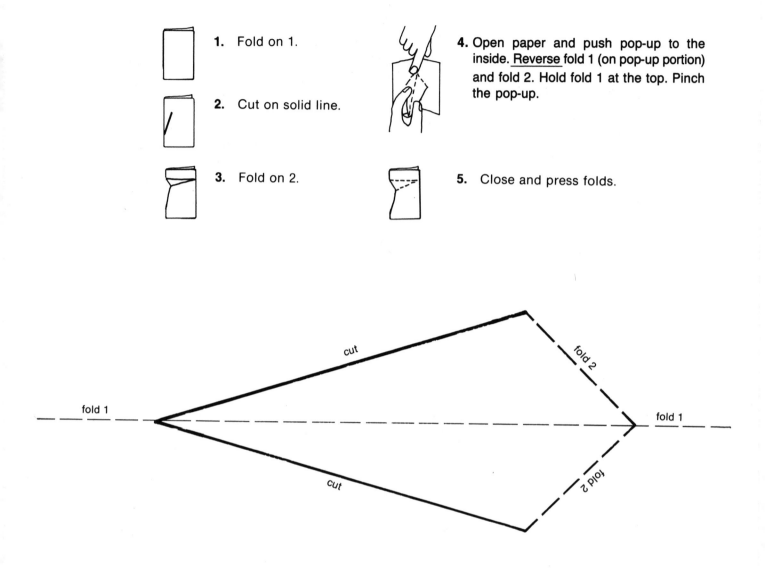

fold 1

cut

fold 2

fold 1

cut

fold 2

Pop-Up Basic Pattern #5

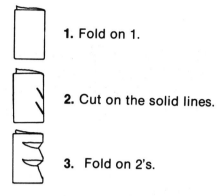

1. Fold on 1.

2. Cut on the solid lines.

3. Fold on 2's.

4. Open the paper and reverse fold 2 by pushing them to the inside.

5. Pinch and pull the pop-up portion from the inside. Close and press the new folds.

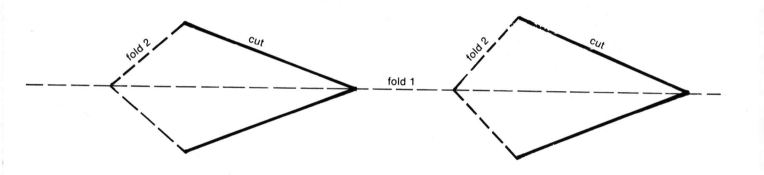

fold 2   cut   fold 1   fold 2   cut

Pop-Up Basic Pattern #6

1. Fold on 1.

2. Cut on solid line.

3. Fold on 2.

4. Open paper and push pop-up to the inside. Reverse fold 1 (on pop-up portion) and fold 2. Hold fold 1 at the top. Pinch the pop-up.

5. Close and press folds.

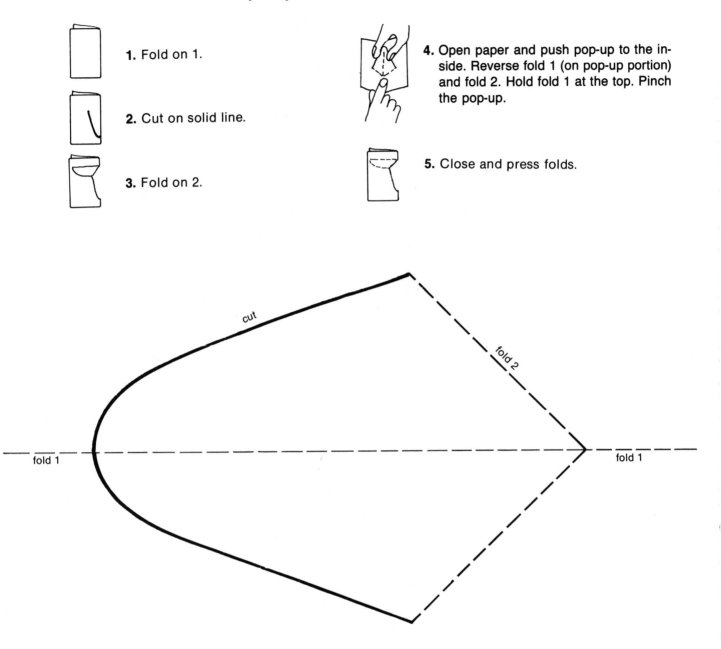

cut

fold 2

fold 1

fold 1

Pop-Up Basic Pattern #7

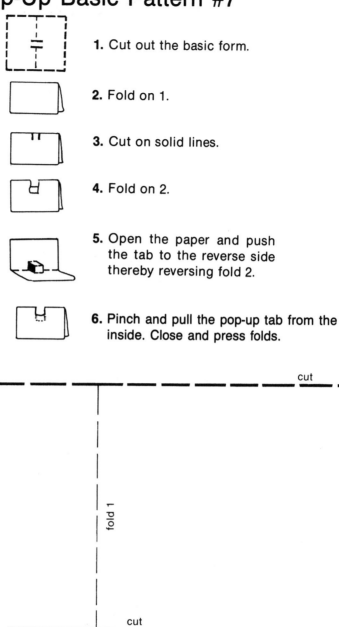

1. Cut out the basic form.

2. Fold on 1.

3. Cut on solid lines.

4. Fold on 2.

5. Open the paper and push the tab to the reverse side thereby reversing fold 2.

6. Pinch and pull the pop-up tab from the inside. Close and press folds.

cut

cut

fold 1

cut

fold 2

cut

fold 1

Pop-Up Basic Pattern #8

1. Fold on 1.

2. Cut on the solid lines.

3. Fold on 2's.

4. Open paper and push the tab to the inside thereby reversing fold 1 and fold 2 on the pop-up portion.

5. Pinch and pull the pop-up tabs from inside. Close and press folds.

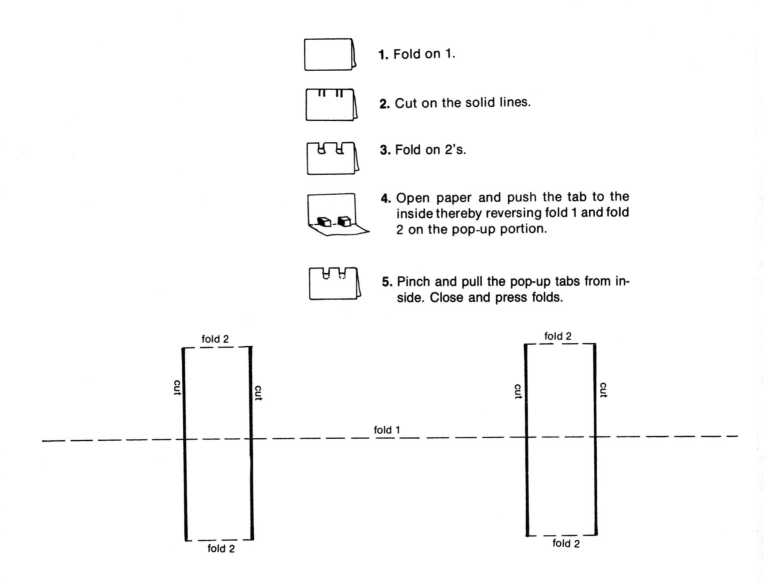